shooti

PHOTOGRAPHS BY

GEORGE BENNETT

shooting POOL

TEXT BY

MIKE SHAMOS

Published in 1998 by Artisan,
a division of Workman Publishing Company, Inc.
708 Broadway, New York, New York 10003

editor: Leslie Stoker
designer: Susi Oberhelman
production director: Hope Koturo

Library of Congress Cataloging-in-Publication Data

Bennett, George, 1945–
     Shooting pool / photographs by George Bennett ;
text by Mike Shamos.
          p.   cm.
     Includes index.
     ISBN 1-885183-95-x

To Robert Byrne, who isn't in this book but should be, for his friendship,
letters and encouragement over the past 15 years. (MIS)

To my wife, Kendall, for her support and
generous acceptance of my enthusiasms. (GB)

CONTENTS

preface   9

THE LEADERS   11

THE WOMEN   35

THE PLACES   55

THE MEN   93

THE INDUSTRY   115

glossary   136

index of names   140

acknowledgments   143

The human race divides itself neatly into two different groups—those who love pool and those who don't. Neither understands the other and often doesn't care to. If you're a pool lover, you'll love this book. If you're not, you won't, but at least you'll begin to understand what it is about pool that pool lovers love.

The book is a view of pool in the United States at the end of the twentieth century as seen through the eyes of one man and described in the words of another. You can look at the pictures or read the words, or both, at your pleasure. It has been our aim to capture the passionate and curious world of pool to gain some insight into what makes so many adults, the author included, devote their lives to pushing balls around a table.

Our approach to selecting material for the book was opportunistic rather than comprehensive. On our travels, if we thought something merited inclusion, George shot it. Only on rare occasions did we go out of our way to include a person or place. If you want to know why a particular individual isn't pictured or why your favorite room isn't here, the answer is simple—we didn't encounter them. The book is also far too short for us to have attempted anything resembling a thorough treatment.

Six months of poking into the pool world produced many thousands of pictures. Some were fine images, but didn't contribute much to the book's overall landscape. After all, how many interesting photos of players posing with cue sticks can there be? The collection was culled, rearranged and ultimately edited down to the hundred or so that follow.

The vocabulary of pool is specialized, mixing ordinary terms with colorful slang. Any word that might be confusing, along with descriptions of common billiard games, can be found in the glossary at the end of the book.

It is reported that the members of certain primitive tribes decline to be photographed out of fear that the camera will steal their souls. I don't know whether the claim is accurate, but they should certainly be afraid of George Bennett. He grabs their essence and spreads it on celluloid. Many of the people he shot for this book I have been acquainted with for years, but I didn't really know them until I saw his pictures. Don't take my word for it—look for yourself.

PREFACE

mike shamos

THE LEADERS

Who is it that changes a field of human endeavor? Is it enough to be good, great or even the best? To be famous, infamous, obnoxious or lovable? No, it is the people who are those who do things differently, and thereby point the way for others. They are the role models, the leaders.

This chapter presents nine leaders of the pool community. You will meet many others throughout the book. Some, like Steve Mizerak and Earl Strickland, are household names. Others, such as Billy Aguero and Ernie Gutierrez, are not. All were chosen because of some unique aspect of their work that has impacted American pool in a substantial way, leaving the game different than it was before they arrived. Mizerak and Strickland are champion players who elevated pool through their tournament performances. Aguero is a house pro who works quietly spreading knowledge about the game. Gutierrez changed the direction of cuemaking. They are single-minded in their dedication to the game. Understand them and you will see what makes the rest of us tick. △

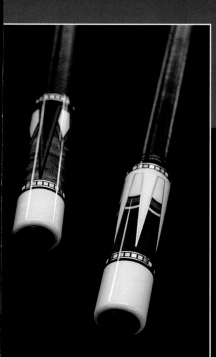

SUE BACKMAN
and BILLY AGUERO

proprietor
and pro

Chalkers house pro Billy Aguero working on his massé technique (previous page).

Billy Aguero practicing the break shot, the most important shot in Nine-Ball (left).

Sue Backman, owner, and Billy Aguero, house pro, at Chalkers San Francisco (below).

Sue Backman owns Chalkers, an upscale room in downtown San Francisco. Originally from Minneapolis, she became fascinated by pool at 13 while visiting friends in Colorado. Her host's handsome son broke his leg, so Backman charitably sacrificed her vacation to shoot pool with him. That same year she saw San Francisco and thought it the best place in the world.

She ran the college coffee house at the University of Minnesota and worked in restaurants before becoming, in succession over the next 20 years, a concert promoter, caterer, pool champion of Telluride, Colorado, food company manager and facilities supervisor for a San Francisco bank. On a brief return visit to Minneapolis in 1988, Backman found her calling. In the space of 24 hours, she (1) played in Shooter's, a local upscale room; (2) read a front-page article on upscale pool; (3) heard a program on National Public radio about upscale pool; and (4) saw a piece in the *New York Times* on upscale pool. The message was clear and it was loud.

On May 3, 1990, Backman, with partner and financial man Peter Hangarter, opened Chalkers in Emeryville, California (just north of Oakland), the first upscale room in the state. She had a comprehensive plan that included a pro shop, instruction, corporate receptions, comfortable atmosphere and a price structure designed to spur business. To discourage hustlers, she forbade loitering. The room, which encouraged both casual and serious players, ultimately expanded to 35 tables.

Though successful in Emeryville, San Francisco was Backman's real objective. She sold the first room (which then changed its name) and opened Chalkers in Rincon Center in December 1993, spending almost a million dollars, all of which is visible in the decor. It has 30 custom tables, three of them in the front row for serious players and a "show-off" table (her words) near the front door. The cloth is all Simonis 860 and the tables are carefully maintained. A pro shop and gourmet kitchen round out Chalkers's amenities. In 1996, Backman became a Senior Writer for *Billiards Digest* magazine, to which she contributes a proprietor's column. She has also served on the Board of Directors of the Billiard Congress of America.

Backman's house pro at Chalkers is Billy Aguero, sometimes known as "Billy the Kid." The house pro is a central figure in a pool room. He makes sure the equipment is in suitable condition, repairs cues, runs the pro shop, attracts good players, gives exhibitions and lessons and runs in-house leagues and tournaments. He's the day manager, greeter, maitre d', and player's friend. An establishment without a pro is at a distinct disadvantage in growing its business.

Aguero started playing when he was 12 at the Boys' Club in San Leandro, California, near Oakland. As he improved, he began playing in nearby Alameda, where he beat progressively better road players who stopped by to challenge him. For years, Aguero made a living playing pool, then played on the pro tour. After becoming a family man, he looked for a more stable situation.

Aguero met Sue Backman in 1992, when he was seeking a sponsor to support him in pro tournaments. He worked some corporate parties for her at Chalkers in Emeryville, and she agreed to back his professional activities, paying his entry fees and expenses in return for a percentage of his winnings. Aguero brought recognition to Chalkers and when her San Francisco room opened, Backman asked him to join as house pro. He charges $40 an hour for lessons, the student paying for table time. Brief lessons are provided free of charge; group clinics are inexpensive.

Now in his forties, Aguero is proud to be able to earn a living as a house pro without having to rely on tournaments or road play. His appetite for professional competition faltered, as did Backman's eagerness to sponsor him, when the PBT failed to pay his prize money after the 1996 U.S. Open Nine-Ball tournament. His present compensation structure ties his fortunes to those of Chalkers. He feels that his success as a house pro depends on the attitude of the owner, which in Chalkers's case is excellent. His attitude toward lessons is simple: "If you teach people something, they come back." △

Billy shooting, Chalkers's bar in foreground.

SHOOTING POOL

the leaders

FRAN CRIMI

master instructor

Fran Crimi outside her teaching room, Corner Billiards at Fourth Avenue and 11th Street in New York City (below).

Crimi begins by evaluating the student's fundamentals during a lesson at Corner Billiards. Here she checks the arm position of Maurice Herman, who operates a building maintenance company and has a pool table in his apartment overlooking Central Park. Coffee is an essential ingredient of Crimi's teaching (left).

Crimi adjusts Herman's stance to ensure that his forearm is perpendicular to the cue stick. The code of ethics for BCA Certified Instructors permits touching a student only with prior permission. In this case, consent was freely given (bottom left).

The only child of an athletic father, Fran Crimi grew up on the streets of Queens, New York, indulging in every sport available. At age 10 she became fascinated by the colors of pool—the green of the cloth and the spectral beauty of the object balls. By 11 she was playing in bars (with her family) but didn't enter a pool room until she was 17. Attracted by the physical challenge of the game, Crimi was determined to excel at it.

While attending Queens College, she won the school's pool title and an entry into the national ACU-I pool tournament, where in 1976 she placed third behind Melissa Rice and Vicki Frechen (now pro Vicki Paski). Frechen was a member of the recently formed WPBA and invited Crimi to play in pro tournaments. In her first event she had the bad luck to be paired against champion Jean Balukas and did not prevail, but Crimi was hooked.

From 1976 until 1990, Crimi was a forensic accountant, involved in such high-profile matters as the tax evasion trial of Leona Helmsley. This allowed her only sporadic tournament play, but she loved teaching and she loved pool. In 1990, she gave up accounting to pursue her dream career as a pool instructor, opening the American Billiard School in New York. It took almost five years for the business to become self-sustaining. She joined the BCA Certified Instructor program at its inception and steadily rose through the ranks. In 1996 she became the eighth (and only female) Master Instructor in the country, which qualifies her to certify other instructors. She now teaches students in the New York area, plays in WPBA tournaments, represents The Schuler Cue, and writes a column for *Billiards Digest*.

The importance of instruction to the future of pool cannot be overestimated. Experience shows that players who continue to improve keep playing. When they stop learning, unless they enjoy the activity for its own sake, and many do, they will drop it in favor of something else. There has long been a tendency for experts, particularly those whose skill is essential to their livelihood, to keep their knowledge secret, and much advanced information has been lost when these people die without having passed on their know-how. Instructional programs run in entirely the opposite direction; their objective is to spread information as widely as possible, and in this Crimi is at the forefront. △

RAY MARTIN

grand master of the cue ball

You can almost tell from the sound of the balls that it's Ray Martin at the table and he's playing Straight Pool. The object ball heads right for the center of the pocket. The cue ball takes two cushions and rolls slowly, stopping precisely where he wants it.

Nine-Ball is fast and flashy; Eight-Ball is a bar game. But Straight Pool requires patience and precision—one mistake can spell death. Almost without exception, the best Straight Pool players are calm souls, able to stay at the table for an hour without missing, running ball after ball and rack after rack. Willie Mosconi, Irving Crane, Luther Lassiter, Nick Varner and Joe Balsis were all world champions who played rhythmically and methodically. Ray Martin is the coolest of them all, hence his nickname: "Cool Cat." How good is he? Martin won three world championships during the 1970s, more than any active player.

Born in New Jersey in 1935, Martin started playing at age 15 and entered his first professional tournament four years later. His first world Straight Pool victory came in 1971, and was repeated in 1974 and 1978. Only two living players, Irving Crane and Jimmy Caras, have won the world championship on more occasions, and they did it when tournaments and challenge matches were held much more frequently. During Martin's career, there was barely one chance each year to win the championship. For his superior play, Martin was inducted into the BCA Hall of Fame in 1994.

How far ahead does Martin plan a run? After a break shot, if all the balls are in the open he knows where he'll pocket every one of them. He won't rush, and is willing to bide his time waiting to eliminate troublesome clusters or reposition a ball for a better break shot. He's also a pool citizen. Some players concentrate on their own careers but leave no legacy other than their record of tournament wins. Martin is the opposite, and a gentleman at the same time. During the 1970s he helped form the Professional Pool Players Association to represent the interests of his fellow pros. In 1977 he wrote a book, *The 99 Critical Shots in Pool*, which is still acclaimed after 20 years, and now contributes a monthly column to *Pool & Billiard Magazine*.

Today, Martin leads a relaxed life in Largo, Florida, giving lessons at home and playing in local tournaments. He rarely travels far to compete, since he's not really fond of Nine-Ball, the current dominant game. "Too much luck," Martin says tersely, "not like Straight Pool." △

the leaders

22

STEVE MIZERAK

just showin' off

Mizerak among some of his many pool products (left).

Mizerak shows the same irreverence today that made him a perfect spokesman for Miller beer (below).

Steve Mizerak is the best-known pool player on the planet. He began play at age four. By 11 he had run 50 at Straight Pool and by 13 he was up to 100. At his first attempt at the world Straight Pool title in 1965, he came in fifth. Starting in 1970, he won the U.S. Open championship four consecutive times, the most victories by any male player, which established him as a superstar, all the while maintaining a career as a high school teacher in New Jersey. He was inducted into the BCA Hall of Fame at age 36 in 1980, the youngest member at the time.

There followed a stint with Miller Brewing Co. for the legendary Miller Lite "Just Showin' Off" commercial in which "The Miz" made three different trick shots in one continuous take with a glass of beer on the table. His attitude and persona meshed perfectly with those of the other Miller athletes, and he was soon signed to a lucrative personal services and appearance contract. The commercial lasted less than half a minute on the air. Interviewed in 1980, Mizerak spoke of its consequences: "Those 29 seconds changed my whole life, in every conceivable way."

His fame spread even further when he won the world title in both 1981 and 1982 and more accolades followed. He was *Billiards Digest* Player of the Year in 1983 and the same year received the Industry Service Award of the Billiard and Bowling Institute of America.

In the 1990s, he organized the Senior Tour, a series of tournaments for players at least 50 years old. The tour has been a success because age in many cases does not diminish billiard skill. Willie Hoppe, for example, retired as world champion when he was 65. Willie Mosconi was able to make long runs at Straight Pool well into his seventies. The Senior Tour players include the game's greats, who are no less interesting to watch than the younger stars.

Today Miz is a walking business. He distributes clothing, supplies and his own line of cues. He gives exhibitions, appears at room openings and stars in instructional videotapes, in addition to running and playing on the Senior Tour. He has co-written nine books on the game. He loves to clown around, but at the table he's deadly serious, as numerous opponents still discover. △

JEAN BALUKAS

superstar

Jean Balukas and father, Al, at her Hall of Fame table (left).

After 30 years in the game, the still-young Balukas regularly runs 60s in Straight Pool (below).

To find the most dominant female pool player in history you have to go to Brooklyn, to the corner of Fifth and Ovington. There you'll find Hall of Fame Billiards, tucked away in peaceful Bay Ridge. It's a family place, with 50 Brunswick tables, run by Al Balukas and his daughter Jean.

On the ground floor is a regular pool room, with a pro shop, vending machines, gold cloth, a Ping-Pong cage, even a lone carom table. But descend below to the basement players' area and you enter a different world. Above each table is a light fixture with the name of a different BCA Hall of Fame member emblazoned in colored glass. It's a gleaming tribute to the game's great players. One of the names you'll see there in lights is that of Jean Balukas.

Jean took up the game very early and at age nine entered the U.S. Open Tournament, finishing fifth out of a field of 17 players. She was fourth in 1970, moved up to third in 1971, then between 1972 and 1983 won the event seven consecutive times. No one else, man or woman, has even come close. Steve Mizerak, with four straight wins, is in second place. Balukas has won the WPBA Nationals six times, twice as many as anyone else, and has been named Player of the Year five times. She used to enter the open division of men's tournaments and finish high in the standings. She is not only the youngest person to be inducted into the Billiard Congress of America Hall of Fame (in 1985), but today, 13 years later, is still its youngest member.

In 1988, however, an incident occurred that led to her estrangement from professional pool. Competing in the Brunswick World Open in Las Vegas, she faced Robin Dodson (then Robin Bell) in a televised semi-final match. Leading 3-2 in a race to 9, Dodson sank the 9-ball twice on successive break shots, prompting Balukas to make an audible comment each time. As Dodson was preparing to break again, Balukas spoke up once more. As a result, Dodson became rattled and Balukas won the next seven games for a 9-5 victory and went on to win the tournament. Dodson finished tied for third and filed a complaint with the Women's Professional Billiard Association (WPBA), which had sanctioned the event.

Balukas's words weren't obscene or even offensive. But they were distracting, and a player has a right under the rules not to have the opponent interfere with the game. The WPBA imposed a modest fine of $200. Balukas refused to pay, not because she felt her behavior was justified, but because her penalty had been determined by the other WPBA players, not an independent body. Once the power to fine a player is in the hands of her opponents, Balukas insisted, fairness goes out the window. In pro football, for example, when a player is ejected for brawling we don't let the opposing team set the fine. The WPBA, its hand forced, disqualified her awaiting payment.

After a mountain of press releases, interviews, editorials and closed-door meetings, Balukas and the WPBA were at an impasse. Lawyers were even engaged, a sure sign of trouble. After five years, the parties quietly reached agreement. Balukas has been eligible to play in women's events ever since. While she supports the WPBA and is friendly with most of its members, she chooses not to devote her time to the rigors of tournament pool, preferring to train for other sports, particularly golf.

Still, questions and rumors abound: What's Jean doing? Is she afraid of competition? Is she still any good? Could she beat Allison Fisher? The answers to the first three are easy: (1) Balukas can still be found playing at Hall of Fame and working the counter; (2) she's not afraid of anybody; and (3) as to how good she is, when photographer George Bennett and I visited her to take pictures for this book, she threw a rack of balls on the table and started to shoot. For the next two hours, through all of our setups, she didn't miss a ball. Can she beat Fisher? Who knows? But we'd all like to see her try. Somebody should give each of them a bag of money to settle the issue the old-fashioned way. Over the table. With cue sticks. △

Jean separated from her championship trophies by a Ping-Pong cage at the family pool room. She hasn't competed professionally since 1988 (right).

Jean Balukas with Tony Meatball, a room regular, outside her family's Hall of Fame Billiards in Brooklyn, New York (below).

EARL STRICKLAND

u.s. champion

Earl Strickland racking Eight-Ball for a challenger who donated $25 to charity to play a single rack with him.

Earl Strickland is one of the three best Nine-Ball players in the world. (Johnny Archer and Efren Reyes are the others.) He is the only person ever to win a million dollars in a single match, which he did by running 11 consecutive racks against Pennsylvania pro Nick Mannino in the first game of the first round of the Professional Cuesports Association's (PCA's) first tournament in 1996, a world record. That's roughly the equivalent of bowling 50 strikes in a row—it had never been done before. In 1997 he again proved supreme by winning the U.S. Nine-Ball Open in Chesapeake, Virginia, for the fourth time.

Strickland is not an easy champion to love. He is moody, temperamental, impatient and loud, often chiding fans for their behavior and drawing fines for his own, in a manner reminiscent of John McEnroe. He is also amazingly talented, enthusiastic, possessed of a wondrous stroke, and one of the most intense competitors in the history of pool. Wherever there is a tournament, if Strickland is there it's a major event.

Strickland typifies the attitude of the U.S. male professionals, who are tremendously skilled and at the same time anxious for success. Originally a PBT stalwart, Strickland was one of the first players to jump to the PCA with C. J. Wiley. These days men's pool is opportunistic; the players go where the money is.

Outside the competitive arena, Strickland can be a perfect gentleman. Before the BCA Trade Expo in Las Vegas in 1997, he agreed, along with a host of other pros, to play in a charity event the night before the show at Pink E's, a large room near the Strip. Earl was the first professional to arrive and the last to leave. He graciously played all challengers for the whole evening and spent the next three days at the trade show cheerfully giving exhibitions. He just loves pool. When his record is toted up, Strickland will prove to be have been one of the most dominating players of the century. △

the leaders

A Blatt craftsman shaping a table leg (right).

Assembling table frames (far right).

RON BLATT

table magnate

When it comes to pool tables, New York is Blatt country. Over the last 75 years, Ron Blatt and his family amassed the largest horde of antique tables in the country. Many are stored in Blatt Billiards' five-story loft at 809 Broadway in Manhattan; others are secreted in undisclosed locations upstate. The extent of the cache is extraordinary—if you're opening a room and need 50 Brunswick Madisons (a model popular 80 years ago), Blatt can supply them.

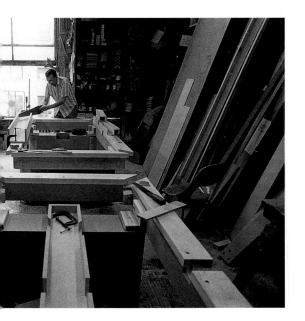

In 1913, Sam Blatt, Ron's grandfather and a cabinetmaker from Russia, came to the United States and began operating a cue repair and ivory turning business out of a storefront near the Brooklyn Bridge. The business was successful; in those days there were more than 2,000 small pool rooms in Manhattan, all of which needed the type of service Blatt offered. Ten years later, he expanded to include selling cloth and repairing tables. As a boy, Ron remembers being covered with buckhorn dust after a day in the workshop. Ferrules then were often made of buckhorn, which is more economical than ivory. When turned on a lathe, buckhorn produces a fine white powder with an unforgettable aroma. By 1960, Ron, then fresh out of school, joined the business full-time. He was struck by the beauty of classic antique tables, particularly their woodwork and decoration and eventually reoriented the business toward acquiring and restoring them.

The first floor of his building is a showroom, but the real work goes on upstairs. There, specialists fashion replacement parts, match veneers, repair damaged parts and painstakingly re-stain century-old wood to bring classic tables back to life.

The value of an antique depends on its rarity, attractiveness and condition. While a brand new top-of-the-line Brunswick Gold Crown can be bought for $4,500, sought-after antiques usually fetch between $12,000 and $50,000, a level that demands a well-heeled clientele. The most expensive table Blatt ever sold went for $145,000, a spectacular Brunswick carved gothic model with three sets of rails (for pool, billiards and snooker) and a matching cue cabinet that looks like a confessional from St. Patrick's Cathedral. The masterpiece is now ensconced, appropriately, in a castle on Long Island. The price was not far from the auction record for a table, which is slightly over $200,000 for an eighteenth-century example with a wooden bed.

There's plenty to admire at Blatt, though, even for the ordinary citizen. He sells modern tables, reproduction models and a line of Blatt custom designs, along with cues and accessories. The wait for a restoration is 6 to 8 months, but new tables are readily available. Though Blatt consistently places among the top ten retailers of Brunswick and Vitalie tables in the country, his contribution to the game is not dollar volume but care and respect for marvelous antiques. △

ERNIE GUTIERREZ

cuemaker extra-ordinaire

Ernie Gutierrez is a self-taught mechanical engineer, machinist and wood turner who came to the United States from Colombia around 1960 and built his first cue in 1961, the year *The Hustler* was released. A few days before the cue was completed, his daughter Gina was born, so he named the cue after her and the Ginacue line was created.

Gutierrez was interested in pool, and began associating with players in the Los Angeles area. Originally he made cues for himself and a few friends, but his sticks began to be used in tournaments, where they stood out in comparison to the simpler styles usual at that time. After he made a silver cue in 1966, orders began to flow in and he was the first cuemaker whose cues passed the invisible $500 price barrier. At one tournament in the late 1960s at Johnston City, Illinois, more than 60 percent of the players were using Ginacues.

In 1973, Gutierrez stopped making cues entirely for 15 years, working instead on Indianapolis race cars and a contract that had him building custom dashboards for Porsche. The renaissance of pool and strikingly elevated prices for collector cues drew him back into cuemaking in 1988 for a second edition of the Ginacue. The most sought-after cue in the country is Ernie's personal ivory and silver design, for which he turned down an offer of $100,000 and a boat!

The unassuming exterior of the Gutierrez workshop in North Hollywood (above).

Cuemaker Ernie Gutierrez at one of his many lathes (left).

Gutierrez operates out of a state-of-the-art workshop in North Hollywood, California. From its unpretentious exterior, you would never know that it contains the latest in computer-controlled lathes and milling machines, some built by Gutierrez himself. He is now content to make 100 to 150 cues a year, all of which are instantly collectible. The process is slow, and he is perpetually backlogged.

The notion of a pool cue as an art form has given rise to a situation in which a stick can easily cost ten times as much as the table on which it is used, making pool unique in this respect: when does a racquet cost more than the tennis court, or a golf club more than the entire course?

THE WOMEN

Women have been playing pool since the 1400s. What's different about the game today is that they're better—much better—than ever before.

Through 1900, women's participation in billiards was largely social rather than serious. During various decades of the nineteenth century, it fell in and out of fashion like hemlines, and play by females was regarded alternately as either genteel or outrageous. After the Civil War, the game was taught in ladies' seminaries. In the 1880s, only a prostitute would consider playing in public. During the Gay Nineties, society's *grandes dames*, including Mrs. Vincent Astor and Mrs. William Vanderbilt, took up the cue with abandon and recommended it to their friends. The game was even touted as improving a woman's figure through constant walking and bending.

With a few exceptions each century, what characterized women's pool until the 1970s was bad, even egregious, play. But who could blame

them? For the first 350 years after the game was invented, women weren't even allowed to use cue sticks, but had to shoot with cumbersome devices called maces. The mace was little more than a heavy wooden block attached to a handle that was used to shove the ball down the table as in shuffleboard. The reason offered for this restriction was that using a cue required a lady to assume an immodest bent-over position, while the mace could be used in an upright posture. The real explanation was that women were presumed to be so incompetent that they would tear the cloth if they used a cue stick, and numerous engravings and cartoons depict them doing just that.

Even a woman who was skilled faced huge obstacles, including ridicule by men, charges of shamelessness from her fellow women, inability to practice in public without harassment and in general a total lack of support for her endeavor, which was regarded as somewhat brazen. Very few were able to persevere. In most cases, those who did were the daughters of billiard room operators, who enjoyed special encouragement and protection. A notable example from this century was Ruth McGinnis (1910–1974), who ran over 100 at Straight Pool and was invited to compete in men's tournaments. But such exceptions did not disprove the rule, and the sight of a woman with a cue was more likely to provoke snide commentary than admiration from either sex.

The modern women's era began with the ascent in the 1970s of Jean Balukas, profiled in the preceding chapter. Here was a woman who displayed athleticism and guts

Lee surveying the table before selecting a shot. Lee combines beauty, a tremendous sense of style, skill and intense determination at the table. Her lengthy practice sessions are literally back-breaking—she suffered from scoliosis of the spine as a child and still fights chronic back problems. Her black outfits and glove are trademarks.

The scene at the final match at the Connelly Classic in Valley Forge, Pennsylvania, in March 1997 between Jeanette Lee (shooting) and Allison Fisher, being televised by ESPN (far right). Every eye in the room is riveted on Lee, a phenomenon that is not difficult to understand. At the left and bottom are VIP and press seats, which provide table space. Regular seating is at the right. The opponent, Allison Fisher, is confined to her chair at the bottom left of the playing area. Everyone else can disturb the shooter, but her opponent cannot.

tournament pool is not easy. The player, alone in a crowd, has to contend with a variety of distractions. The lighting is not ordinary table lighting, but comes from floodlights required for television. Instead of being suspended directly over the table as usual, the lights surround it and are angled toward the table, causing glare in the shooter's eyes. Camera work is done by a roving band of men with hand-held cameras, more concerned with getting good shots than staying out of the players' way.

The spectators at such events are usually well-informed and well-behaved. Unlike everyone else in the arena, they're not there to make money, but to enjoy some good pool.

the referee's most important function is to judge fouls. Because of budgetary constraints, officiating at pool events in this country is usually not performed by a professional staff of referees, but is a task doled out to friends of the tournament promoter, who often are not conversant with the rules.

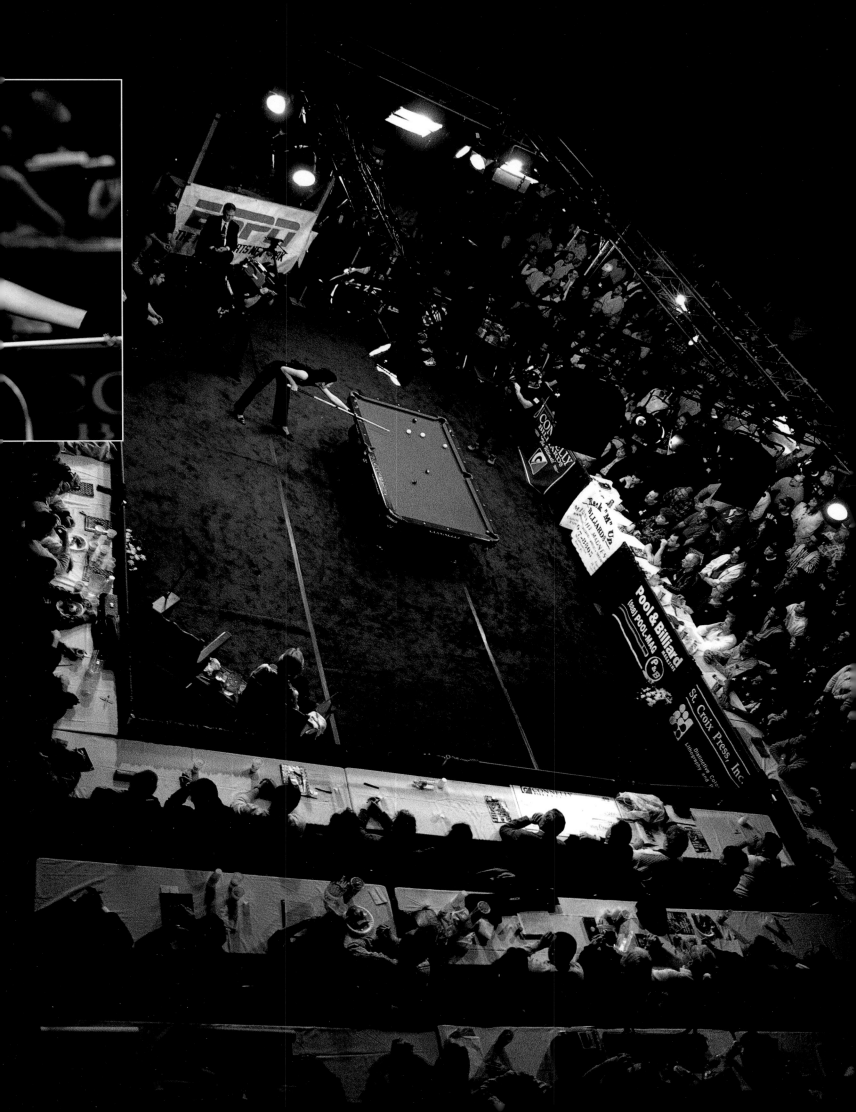

and could beat men on equal terms. When pool revived in the late 1980s, Balukas served as a model for a whole generation of female players. After upscale rooms began to appear, it was no longer socially questionable for women to play in public. Those with enough drive and ability became good, often seeking instruction and coaching guidance from male professionals. The turning point came in 1976 with the formation of the Women's Professional Billiard Alliance (WPBA, later renamed the Women's Professional Billiards Association) by Palmer Byrd and Madeline Whitlow. With Billie Billing as its first President, the WPBA agitated for the establishment of women's divisions in major tournaments.

By 1993, the collection of women pros was skilled and diverse enough for the establishment of the Classic Tour, an annual series of regular sponsored tournaments, many of which are televised. The women understand what the men apparently do not, that commercial success requires offering an entertaining product. The WPBA imposes dress and behavior codes and is able to put on an appealing show that attracts sponsors. More than that, the players offer each other various forms of support, from playing advice to business tips and plain friendship, all of which strengthens the organization. It

in Snooker, the pockets are very narrow and a ball that is not headed for the center of a pocket is likely not to go in. Pockets on American tables are much wider, and will accept a ball even if it arrives considerably off-center. Nine-Ball players depend on this effect to position the cue ball. If the cue ball and object ball are lined up directly with a pocket, a Snooker player has little choice other than to draw ("screw" in British parlance) the cue ball back or allow it to follow forward. If a Nine-Ball player wants to send the cue ball off to the left after the shot, all she need do is aim the object ball slightly to the right side of the pocket. It will still drop, and the cue ball will head off in the desired direction. Fisher is still learning to make full use of this technique, which is unfamiliar in Snooker.

Allison Fisher chalks her cue under the gaze of an ESPN cameraman during her match with Jeanette Lee. Calmness and confidence from her successful Snooker career led Fisher to total dominance over the 1997 WPBA Classic Tour. She has an uncanny ability to send balls directly toward the center of the pocket. Curiously, this was initially a drawback to her Nine-Ball game.

Considerably shorter than Lee, Fisher must often lean far over the table with a leg draped on the rail. Here she is stretched out to the maximum and uses the open-hand bridge common in snooker. A closed-hand loop bridge would be impossible in this stance. Tall players have an advantage because they are able to reach more shots without leaning so far over. Shooting while leaning on the table bed must be practiced; the player's weight shifts differently during the stroke in that position and can result in a miss even if the cue stick is initially aimed properly.

would be simple to claim that the appeal of women's pool for men is watching pretty women bend over the table, but that's not what it's about. Some of the WPBA players are beautiful; some aren't. Some are extraordinary players; some aren't. But all of them are driven; they love pool and it shows in their play.

The women have organized into a coherent tour that has no competitors. They encourage one another and spend substantial time with their fans. By comparison, men's pool resembles a civil war. While the men are excellent players, they have not yet found the right formula to secure commercial sponsorship, while the WPBA is able to raise more money every year.

This chapter shows the WPBA pros as they appeared at the Connelly Classic, a tournament held at Allen and Dawn Hopkins's Super Billiards Expo in Valley Forge, Pennsylvania, in March 1997. The 47 entries included all of the top-ranked women, and the three-day competition was intense. The battle shaped up among Allison Fisher, Jeanette Lee, Vivian Villarreal and Robin Dodson.

A players' meeting is held before every tournament to review the rules and announce initial pairings. From left to right are WPBA pros Aileen Pippin, Nesli O'Hare, Loree Jon Jones, Ewa Laurance, Peg Ledman, Allison Fisher, Mary Guarino and Gerda Hofstatter (below).

WPBA President Ewa (pronounced Eva) Mataya Laurance, a native of Sweden, is a major contributor to women's pool through talk show appearances, exhibitions, promotional work for Brunswick, television announcing and as author of *The Ewa Mataya Pool Guide* (Avon, 1994). Originally married to professional pool player Jimmy Mataya, her determination and charisma propelled her both to a top player ranking and an appearance on the cover of the *New York Times Magazine* in 1992. She holds the women's U.S. Open Straight Pool high run record of 68. Ewa is now married to actor Mitchell Laurance ("L.A. Law"). The pair can often be seen calling play-by-play for ESPN.

Laurance in an early round of the tournament. Because of the number of entries, many matches must be played simultaneously (overleaf).

The lag for break in the first game of the Fisher-Villarreal match (above).

The competitors watch carefully as the balls return (right).

Fisher is pleased to have won the lag, which gives her the chance to draw first blood. Villarreal is consigned to her chair. Pool is one of the few games in which a player can keep her opponent out of the game indefinitely. In this respect it differs from tennis, golf, basketball, baseball, volleyball, archery and most other individual and team sports (far right).

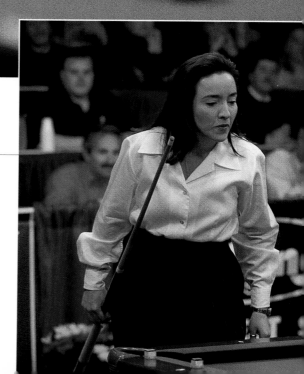

In **lag for break** the players simultaneously shoot an object ball down the length of the table and back. The one whose ball stops closest to the cushion is the winner and is given the option to break. A cue ball is not used during the lag since the player who shot it would have a slight advantage from being accustomed to hitting the cue ball. Sometimes two cue balls are employed to be fair to both players, but here the 1-ball and 5-ball were used. No one passes up the break. If the 9-ball goes in a pocket, the breaker wins in a single shot. If any other ball goes in, the player has a chance to run the table to win the game.

A relative latecomer to pool who did not start playing until in her teens, Dodson, born in 1956, spent time on the road learning the game. She picked up fine points from famous hustlers at the Billiard Palace in Bellflower, California, and was that state's champion in the 1970s. She turned professional in 1984, was 1991 Player of the Year and finished first in the WPBA in 1995. Dodson credits her success to religion and uses a custom cue bearing an inlaid cross.

Villarreal, born in 1965, was the game's leading U.S. female money-winner in 1996. Her record earnings of $120,450 exceeded those of all but two male pool players. An all-around athlete, she learned to play at age eight and has usually been ranked in the top four in the WPBA since her first tournament win in 1991 in Honolulu. She was named Player of the Year in 1992. Based in San Antonio, Villarreal won $60,000 in a single tournament (the ESPN World Open) in 1996, also a record.

Lee, born in 1971, is a native of New York who began playing as a teenager in Queens. She wore black clothing exclusively and became known as the "Black Widow"—as much for her deadly accuracy as her dark hair and outfits. Though sought after as a model, Lee was determined to become the best player in the world and toward that end practiced between 10 and 12 hours a day. After joining the pro tour in 1992, it took her only two years to achieve a #1 ranking. Winning half the events on the Classic Tour in 1994 earned her Player of the Year honors. Lee, now married to professional pool player George Breedlove and based in Long Beach, California, is ranked second in the world to Allison Fisher.

Fisher, a blonde transplant from England who began playing at age seven, became National Ladies Champion at 15 and was Women's World Snooker champion seven times before moving to the United States in 1995 when the prospects for women's snooker in Britain had grown dim. She rose quickly to the top of the WPBA rankings, becoming Player of the Year in 1996. In 1997 she had the Classic Tour in a stranglehold, winning the majority of its tournaments, including a streak of seven consecutive victories. △

Villarreal reviews the match in her head. There were many shots on which the outcome could have hinged (left).

Just another day at the office. Fisher unscrews to await her final opponent (below).

Lee sometimes practices ten hours a day. At exhibitions, she gives an inspirational speech explaining why. "I want to be the best in the world. I was walking down the street one day and I realized that I wasn't playing but my potential opponents might be. How can I be the best in the world unless I practice more than they do?" The playing form of the top women is exceptional. By contrast, many of the best men exhibit bad playing habits that they have learned to overcome with experience. Here Lee has the cue stick positioned directly under her chin, which, despite her height, she has brought down low enough to sight the shot properly. Unable to make a full closed-hand bridge on the table bed because the rail is in her way, Lee rests her forearm on the rail while using her last two fingers for support. The purpose of the glove, aside from intimidating opponents, is to keep the cue stick moving smoothly through her bridge hand.

Lee took the match to 6–5 but could not overcome Fisher in the last game. Fisher ran out from the 2-ball to win the event. Lee, seated in the corner, knows what is about to come (overleaf).

After this performance, a brief celebration is in order (above).

Fisher indulges herself with a look of guilty pleasure after the win (left).

Minutes later, a fully composed Fisher accepts the championship trophy as Allen and Dawn Hopkins, the event organizers, look on (right).

UEBLEF

Vorld's Finest Cue

THE PLACES

The pool room. Just the term itself
was once enough to strike fear in the hearts of mothers everywhere.
Imagining what evils their sons might encounter in them (daughters
would never even consider entering one) gave women palpitations. In
the 1920s, the country's largest table manufacturer, the Brunswick-
Balke-Collender Company, used this phenomenon in a brilliant stroke
of advertising hocus-pocus. Pool halls were so noxious, the idea went,
that the way to keep children out of them was to buy a table for the
house! It even offered a line of models called "The Home Magnet," so
attractive to adolescents they would be drawn magically back into the
house for a game of pool should they ever be tempted to go out.

However many home tables might have been sold through this
ruse, it did not diminish the number of pool rooms. Just as poker with
the boys isn't so much fun with the wife and kids around, men needed
to retreat to the grimy sanctity of the pool hall to smoke, drink and play

a little "money ball," activities that did not engender a healthy relationship with municipal authorities. Ordinances exist in various towns that ban public pool-playing entirely, keep it away from churches, forbid minors to play, forbid hard liquor, impose a curfew of 9:00 p.m., subject proprietors to moral scrutiny and allow police to enter at any time without having to provide justification. In many states the laws restricting pool playing can be found in the statute books right next to those banning prostitution and other vices.

The courts have uniformly upheld such regulations as necessary for the public good. In 1902, a judge in Nebraska declared solemnly that "A pool room in a village is apt to degenerate into a tryst for idlers and a nidus for vice." "Nidus" means something worse than you probably imagine. It's a "nest or breeding place where bacteria or other organisms lodge and multiply." That's quite an indictment, to compare an innocent game in which balls are rolled around on a table to an infectious disease.

It would be nice to dismiss the Nebraska decision as turn-of-the-century lunacy. However, the century is about to turn again, and the lunacy has not fully abated. In 1997, former world Three-Cushion champion Sang Lee was denied an occupancy permit for a new room in Lincolnwood, a presumably morally erect community not far from Chicago. What its citizens lost by not having the greatest player in North and South America in their town will undoubtedly be another community's gain. For pool will be played somewhere, regardless of local efforts to suppress it.

The ambience of the locale affects the quality of play and the enjoyment of the game for participants and spectators alike. This is true whether the location is a bar, poolroom, private club, YMCA or the family basement. The range of places in which pool is played spans the entire

Jillian's in Long Beach, California, looks more like a bank than a pool room. It should. The building actually was once a bank (below). A conglomerate of franchises that started in Boston around 1990, Jillian's was the first room chain to hold an initial public stock offering.

Jillian's ceiling ornamentation and rich polished wood lend an antique air to one of the country's most beautiful rooms (right).

spectrum of society, which means that you can find anything if you go out looking for it.

For some players, equipment is paramount. They're perturbed if the table is not exactly level, the cloth is too slow or balls don't drop cleanly into the pockets. These people seek out a "players' room," one that caters to serious pool players while relegating to second place (or no place) such amenities as food and decor. Others seek out opportunities for gambling, regardless of the caliber of player or equipment they might find. They're looking for an "action room" where betting is a virtual necessity. Some of the best action rooms are understandably also players' rooms—if you're wagering a lot of money on a game, you don't want to lose because the rails aren't tight.

Which brings us to a forbidden topic—gambling. Some industry leaders believe that if the public finds out that people bet money on pool games a crack will open in the ground and we'll all be sucked into oblivion, sponsors will disappear, television will cancel its contracts and the game will be outlawed by nervous politicians anxious to deflect attention from themselves. Others aren't sure, but declare that no good can come of airing the game's dirty laundry.

The purpose of this book is to show pool as it actually is, not the way well-meaning people wish it might be. Betting on pool games is widespread in the United States. It's rampant in San Francisco, *sub rosa* in Pittsburgh and flagrant in Philadelphia. Some games engender it—only the Easter Bunny plays One-Pocket for fun. Three-Cushion players have no need of it; the beauty of the game seems satisfaction enough. Wagering on one's own game is sometimes legal; betting on the performance of others is not. How proprietors deal with the phenomenon varies. Some rooms eject gamblers, others tolerate them. Some places encourage them, for they represent a steady source of business. Occasionally the owner becomes so involved in it he makes book on games in his own room and holds the stake for the players, risking the room's license every time he does! At every tournament spectators can be seen betting, but the same can be said of every baseball, football, basketball and hockey game.

The real problem arises when professionals in public matches deliberately lose to create an advantage for certain bettors, a practice known as "dumping,"

The private rooms at the HAC are more luxurious than most hotels (above).

The Hollywood Athletic Club (which actually *was* an Athletic Club in the 1930s) stands at the corner of Sunset and Cherokee. HAC features a highly acclaimed restaurant, Drones Bar & Grill, and attracts the expected crowd of Hollywood glitterati (right).

Hollywood Athletic Club
RESTAURANT BAR & BILLIARDS
LIVE MUSIC
DANCING

Sunset
6500 W
Bl

or agree in advance with other competitors to share winnings as an insurance policy against losing, called "saving." If anything has the capacity to destroy the interest of sponsors and attract the attention of law enforcement (not to say organized crime), this is it.

If you need to know, yes, there are pictures of hustlers in this book. They're not identified. But that merely reinforces a point: hustlers are ordinary people. They don't bear the mark of Cain and part of their danger is that you can't tell who they are just by looking.

It's quite possible to shoot pool for years without ever seeing or being involved in gambling, though selective blindness may be helpful. Large numbers of rooms appeal to players searching for fun, a chance to be sociable or a way to show off their limited pool skills to an appreciative audience who know even less than they do about the game. An increasing number of "yuppie" or "upscale" rooms solicit this audience. These are places in which attractive surroundings, good food and drink, throbbing music, a large population of singles and elevated

Gotham Hall in Santa Monica, California, is one of the most stylish rooms in the country. Owned by Rene Mizrahi, Isaac Mizrahi's sister, it is proof that taste runs in the family. The interior space is unmolested by vertical columns, the bugaboo of the pool player.

The **purple** cloth, which may seem shocking at first, has a sound historical basis. For five centuries, until the 1930s, green was the universal color of billiard cloth. The choice appears to date back to the fifteenth century, when billiards, originally an outdoor lawn game, was brought indoors and moved up onto a table. Green was used to simulate the appearance of grass. So religious was the attachment to green that no other color was ever mentioned in previous billiard literature dating back to 1674.

green became indelibly associated with pool rooms. Anyone passing a room would see large pools of green light emanating from the tables and reflected on the ceiling. There have been times, occurring at fairly regular intervals over the last 150 years, in which pool has been declared a corrupter of men and a scourge to the youth of the country. At such times, the billiard industry has looked frantically for ways to counteract this negative image.

During the 1930s, Brunswick, then as now the largest billiard manufacturer in the United States, tried to erase the evil connotation of the color green by introducing purple cloth at the 1935 World Three-Cushion Championship. The effort was unsuccessful, probably because of purists who felt that pool just wasn't pool if played on a cloth other than green. Now that visual impressions have risen in importance, maybe purple, regal color that it is, will find acceptance.

Hollywood Billiards is a players' room. It attracts money players, which means the equipment has to be good and the atmosphere conducive to serious pool. The artwork on the walls is a bonus. Why is it called Hollywood Billiards even though it's in San Francisco? It's owned by the same group that operates Hollywood Billiards in Los Angeles.

Hollywood Billiards sits on a busy street in downtown San Francisco. Originally Cochran's in the 1940s but closed for many years, the room was resurrected as the Q Club by player Tony Annigoni in the early 1990s. Annigoni's life as a road player was detailed in the book *Playing Off the Rail*, by David McCumber (Random House, 1996). McCumber withdrew a playing stake of $40,000 from his savings account and traveled with Annigoni for four months, largely by rail (one of the title's multiple meanings), acting as his playing partner, backer and confessor. The pair got themselves in and out of a succession of tight situations trying to make money at the table. At times, their quest for the anonymity so essential to the perfect hustle backfired completely. When Annigoni walked into Breakers, the top action room in Pittsburgh, in November 1994, hoping for a big score, he hadn't taken five steps before someone yelled out, "Hey, Annigoni, wasn't that you in the tournament in Akron last week?"

table rates generally take precedence over the requirements of fine play. You can find a good time in them, but you'll want to go elsewhere to practice for the U.S. Open.

Yet another segment of the pool population heads for bars and taverns to hoist a pitcher and knock the balls around on a quarter table with an occasional break for square dancing or a fistfight. (Crimes do occur in pool halls once in a while, but it appears to the author that they're disproportionately reported. Serious felonies in bars attract no journalistic interest, but if a punch is thrown in a pool hall it always makes the paper.)

Stereotypes may be accurate in the aggregate but are almost always unfair in individual cases. Many upscale rooms host excellent players and count professionals among their regulars. Some taverns have never suffered a brawl and are able to field championship bar-league teams. And there are action rooms so genteel you would never know thousands of dollars are changing hands every hour without a lesson in how to spot the telltale signs. This chapter contains visual vignettes from about 30 rooms around the country, and you can find at least one of each different type described above. Together they provide an overview of contemporary pool in the United States. △

Blue Fin Cafe and Billiards in Monterey, California, has an address on Cannery Row and a spectacular view of Monterey Bay. The scenery is so nice that some players report they would rather look at the ocean than concentrate on the game. Tony Annigoni (above) is in charge of Blue Fin's marketing.

Sun streams in the Blue Fin's windows. Pool players are not out this early in the day. In a memorable scene from the 1961 film *The Hustler*, after an all-night session between Minnesota Fats (Jackie Gleason) and Eddie Felson (Paul Newman), a room employee at Ames Billiards dares to open the blinds to let in the morning light and Fats immediately yells, "Cut out that lousy sunshine!" There's a good reason to keep sunlight out of a pool room. The player's attention must be focused on the playing surface of the table, which should be the brightest object in the room. Other light is distracting and can cause uneven table illumination, which has an effect on aiming. There's also a physiological factor. Many pool players are creatures of the night, to whom sunlight is as welcome as it would be to a vampire (overleaf).

Monterey has one of the highest densities of upscale rooms in the country. Monterey Billiards (above) and Bow Tie Billiards provide competition for Blue Fin in what is basically a small town.

Meeker Vineyards is located in Healdsburg, Sonoma County, in the heart of the California wine country. General manager and winemaker Mike Loykasek loves pool. Every year, he creates a wine label with a pool theme and an outrageous pun. Shown from left to right are his wines from 1991 through 1996. The 1991 Zinfandel shows a red table and is simply called "red table wine." Another label, "Break Time," has two cue sticks and two broken glasses. Two bulls holding pool cues adorn "Table Stakes." Other animals are used for "Wild Game" and "Rack of Lamb." A sign in the tasting room reads, "Little Bo-Poop had a wayward sheep, Who played pool almost every day, Two bulls that he knew, Who were handier with the cue, Taught him hiding from Bo doesn't pay. If you have any questions or are just lonely and want to talk, you can call us at 407-431-2148. Thanks!"

Bar leagues thrive in Sonoma County. Red's Recovery Room is a supporter of tavern pool, which is Eight-Ball played on seven-foot coin-operated tables. Red's has only four tables, and pool is often free. More than a million people in the United States participate in bar leagues, which combine social drinking and competitive pool with a heavy dose of fun.

The arch rival of Red's is the Wagon Wheel Saloon. A supporter of the North Bay Pool League, its success is demonstrated by a line of trophies mounted on the ceiling (below).

The 8 Ball, neatly tucked away among the trees of northern California, is a member of the same league (right).

Gold Rush Billiards is not a tavern, but a serious players' room in Santa Rosa, California. Don't be misled by the signs offering tattoos and bail bonds. Though at one time these would have been indispensable services in some of the nation's pool rooms, at Gold Rush they're just there as free advertising for the sponsors of the room's in-house league. Some pool fans are known to sport elaborate tattoos, however.

Fat Kat's exhibits the sleek look of a new Miami room (right).

Billiards is immensely popular among Latins everywhere, especially in South Florida. Hernando Piñeres, a large, affable Colombian, is one of the country's greatest billiard enthusiasts. His New Wave Billiards in southwest Miami is the center of Three-Cushion billiards in the southeastern United States. His tournaments draw players from all over the country as well as Central and South America.

In 1995, Hernando Piñeres took a telephone call from a stranger who was looking for a billiard room in which to host a course on **artistic billiards** to be taught over a five-day period by Hans de Jager, a former European champion. Artistic Billiards is very hard on the table because of the powerful massé strokes employed. This damage is particularly severe when it is played by beginners, and the cloth always needs replacement after a session of any length. Hernando's tables are Wilhelminas, one of the best heated carom models with two-inch slates and Simonis Super Roulant cloth, among the fastest on Earth. The stranger asked if Hernando would dedicate one of his tables for a week to five players he didn't know. Of course Hernando said yes. And not only did he allow two tables at New Wave to be used, he invited all of the students to play on his Belgian Van Laare at home! The caller with this unusual request was the author, who has ever since been grateful for Hernando's hospitality and enthusiasm for billiards.

Pete Rose's room in Boca Raton displays a passion for pool and a longing for baseball. The connection between the games has always been close.

Many **major league baseball players** were billiards players; some excelled at both. Almost a century ago, Cap Anson was as well known in billiards as he was in baseball, and catcher Johnny Kling, who also owned a famous room in Kansas City, even won the national pool championship in 1909. In those days, teams traveled by rail. The 1916 Chicago Cubs had a pool table installed in their private car to alleviate boredom on long trips. Babe Ruth sometimes played at charity benefits.

The gambling that caused Pete Rose's demise in professional baseball would have made him a hero in pool, or at the very least would have been accepted as a financial necessity. The world of baseball is tightly controlled and organized; by comparison professional pool is a relative free-for-all.

pool rooms have a long tradition of offering services other than billiards. Among the most common adjuncts are the restaurant, the bowling alley and the video arcade. Other combinations can also be found. One of the most unusual is at Franklin's Sporting Goods in Aliquippa, Pennsylvania, downstream on the Ohio River about 30 miles from Pittsburgh. The front part of the store is dedicated to bait and fishing tackle. The rear is a pool room with classic Brunswick tables and cues from the 1940s. The sign "Pool Players Only in this Area" is somewhat enigmatic—one meaning, probably unintended, is that pool shooters must stay away from the fishing gear. But the two sports share some common history. A hundred years ago, Brunswick was a major supplier of both billiard and fishing equipment. While studying some old Brunswick supply catalogs, Victor Stein, author of *The Billiard Encyclopedia*, realized that Irish linen, one of the standard materials used for wrapping pool cues, was also sold by Brunswick for fishing line.

In most states, it's permissible to conduct an otherwise legal business out of a pool hall. Not in Alaska. Section 23.15.420 of the Alaska Statutes makes it illegal to "conduct an employment agency . . . in connection with a pool hall." So in Alaska if you need a job you had better not look for one in the local pool room. But who would anyway?

Only half an hour but a world away from Franklin's is the Duquesne Club, Pittsburgh's exclusive bastion of Fortune 500 executives. For a hundred years it has maintained one of the most beautiful club rooms in the country. The paintings on the walls are original oils; the one at center is *The Retrievers* (1863) by British artist George Horlor. The players (left to right) are Michael DeMarco, Dan Crawford, Frederick Ziesenheim, and David Simpson, all numbered among Pittsburgh's business elite.

Since the 1890s, private clubs have played an important role in amateur pool and billiards by fielding intercity teams and hosting national tournaments. A hub of such activity is the New York Athletic Club, which employs a full-time billiard room manager, Isa Ismaili. One of its former members, Edward Lee, was many times U.S. Amateur Three-Cushion Champion, winning his first title in 1931 and his last in 1964(!). In 1936 he won the World Amateur crown. Lee and World Professional Champion Willie Hoppe appeared in a 1952 movie, *The Willie Hoppe Story*, which was filmed at the New York Athletic Club. The club maintains an active league program run by a committee known as the Knights of the Green Table, led by member Mike Stap. Overlooking Central Park, the club's billiard room enjoys one of the best views in the United States (overleaf).

Oriental players are helping to keep carom games flourishing in this country, and oriental rooms are still springing up in New York. 4 x 4 Billiards in Flushing held its grand opening in July 1997. Here some Korean players are indulging in Four-Ball, a form of the game never played by Westerners. The object is to make one of the white balls hit the two red balls without touching the other white. Varying numbers of cushions must be hit on different shots throughout the game, and scoring is complex (above).

Numerical handicaps in **four-ball** are assigned based on the player's skill. At 4 x 4, the sign on the wall in Korean reads, roughly, "If your handicap is less than 300, please do not play massé shots." This warning reflects the nearly universal (and somewhat justified) fear among roomkeepers that indiscriminate practice of massé shots by novice players will result in destruction of the cloth. A good cloth now costs about $250, so their skittishness is understandable.

three-cushion billiards owes its survival in the United States in large measure to Asians and Latinos. Dormant for decades, this exquisite game had no more than a few thousand active players in this country until Korean champion Sang Chun Lee moved to New York in the 1980s with the goal of winning the world championship (which he did in 1993). He honed his skills at Abel's Club in Astoria, New York, run by billiard aficionado and jewelry designer Abel Calderone, then opened his own room, SL Billiards, on Roosevelt Avenue in Elmhurst, a section of Queens. The neighborhood is so diverse that you have to look closely to find the room, crowded as it is between immigration lawyers and karaoke parlors. Between 1991 and 1995, nearly 13,000 people moved there from 123 different countries, in some of which billiards is a national mania.

SL Billiards quickly drew the best players in the area. It is a hub of three-cushion activity, a place where race and cultures mix freely and one can always find several of the country's finest players. At 11:00 a.m. on a Saturday in July, a time when the floor is still being swept in other rooms, each of its seven tournament Verhoeven carom tables was busy. Why? Few rooms offer better players, better equipment or better maintenance. The tables are vacuumed and a fresh set of balls provided after every game. (Some pool rooms don't even own a vacuum cleaner and can't imagine what difference it makes if the balls are dirty. They'll never find out since no one who knows would ever play in them.) The most common source of soiling on balls is a film of billiard chalk, which plays havoc with the angle at which they rebound, a critical factor in Three-Cushions, since the balls sometimes must travel over 30 feet to complete a shot.

Danny Rhee, Mike Kang and Sonny Cho (left to right), three of the 15 top-ranked players in the United States at SL Billiards on a Saturday morning to practice for the 1977 U.S. National tournament. Their regimen must have worked: Kang came in second (to Sang Lee); Cho finished fourth; Rhee barely missed qualifying for the finals (below).

The row of painted railbirds gracing Old Princeton Landing,
a waterfront tavern near Half Moon Bay, California, ensures
an enthusiastic audience at all hours (above).

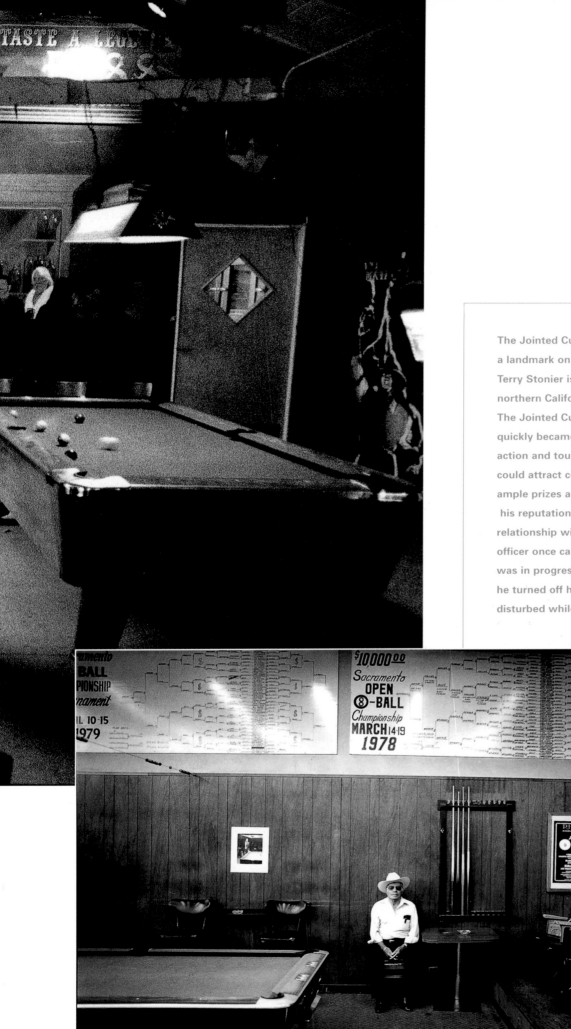

The Jointed Cue in Sacramento, California, is a landmark on any pool player's map. Owner Terry Stonier is a legend who kept pool alive in northern California during the difficult 1970s. The Jointed Cue opened in the 1960s and quickly became known as the state's primary action and tournament room. Stonier realized he could attract competitors with good equipment, ample prizes and a tournament facility, and his reputation grew. He also has an exceptional relationship with the local police (below). An officer once came in while a high-stakes game was in progress. Instead of making an arrest, he turned off his walkie-talkie so as not to be disturbed while watching the match!

laura shepard represents the new breed of professional women taking to pool in a serious way. She has worked at a stock brokerage, traveled around the world, obtained an MBA at Carnegie Mellon University and now works for a high-tech company in Silicon Valley. Her leisure time is devoted to pool. It's her Zen, she says: "Some people meditate, others paint. I shoot pool."

Shepard is tall, skillful and confident, a lot to handle for the typical male player. She confesses to amusement at deflating the egos of men who think that women can't play pool. At Shootz she was able to beat most of the men, other than house pro and tour professional J. R. Calvert. She loves the camaraderie of the contemporary pool world, how players are generally friendly, mutually supportive and willing to share playing tips.

When asked what gender barriers she had encountered in taking up pool, Shepard immediately offered this response: "I think any woman who can hold a cue the right way has had this problem— some guy who couldn't beat you on your worst day has been watching your game and feels it's his right and duty to explain some point of the game. This is totally unsolicited, and I've never figured out why it happens, but it's really annoying."

Laura Shepard assembling her cue at Shootz Cafe & Billiards in Pittsburgh, Pennsylvania, the city's only upscale room.

South of the Monongahela River in the Dormont section of Pittsburgh, and only a few miles from Shootz, is Breakers, a prominent players' room. The equipment is perfect and the atmosphere 100 percent pool. It draws many regulars, like Steve Evans (above), who can often be seen there on weekday afternoons.

Southwest of Breakers is South Hills Golden Cue in Bridgeville, Pennsylvania. The owner, Jimmy Marino, was the best pool player in the country in 1971 and has a trophy from the World All-Round Tournament in Johnston City, Illinois, to prove it. "Hippie Jimmy," as he was known then for his long hair, beat Luther Lassiter to take the undisputed Nine-Ball title and went on to finish first in the all-round category, which included Straight Pool and One-Pocket. Aside from making him look like a war protester, Marino's hair caused some problems at the table. In a tournament he was once called for a foul when his hair accidentally touched a ball. Marino is also a Three-Cushion player of some distinction. His South Hills room, which has an amphitheatre for spectators, is a favorite among young players.

BILLIARD GAME RULES

29

new york has been a major billiard center since the 1820s, when the first pool rooms were organized. Before then, pool was played publicly in taverns, usually on a single table, or in private homes. The rise of the pool hall started slowly, then accelerated tremendously beginning in the 1880s. By 1930, there were over 3,000 licensed pool establishments in Manhattan alone. The number declined drastically after World War II, and was down to a mere handful in 1985, when public pool in New York was threatened by extinction.

The renaissance in upscale rooms began in 1987 with the opening of Chelsea Billiards on 20th Street, in a retail and light manufacturing neighborhood in which zoning presented no problem. Other areas of Manhattan were less receptive to the game; as a result, the Chelsea district now boasts the heaviest concentration of pool rooms in the United States. All of the establishments pictured can be found within a radius of 500 yards. Julian's, alas, one of New York's oldest and seediest parlors, closed for good in 1997, and all of its tables and fixtures were auctioned.

amsterdam billiards has become the focal point of New York pool. Opened by Comedian David Brenner in 1990, locations on both Manhattan's Upper West Side and Upper East Side now attract prime players and stage important events, such as the 1997 WPBA Brunswick New York Classic, won by Allison Fisher. Before his death in 1996, Hall of Fame member Cisero Murphy, the most accomplished African-American player in U.S. history, played regularly at Amsterdam.

Amsterdam prides itself on customer service. House man Rolando Aravena repairs equipment, recommends cues, organizes tournaments, conducts free instructional clinics and generally stirs up enthusiasm. His in-house leagues draw an astounding 300 players. It's also the site of such important tournaments as the Brunswick New York Classic. Because of its status as New York's showcase room, Amsterdam can draw celebrities—Bruce Willis, Paul Sorvino, Jerry Seinfeld, NHL star Mark Messier, Jerry Orbach, Michael Douglas, Martin Short and Steve Martin all have been seen playing there. Watch out for Orbach, star of NBC's "Law and Order." He's one the best actor-players in the country.

Owner-comedian David Brenner and Manager Ethan Hunt enter their fashionable room on Manhattan's Upper East Side.

The future of pool depends on bringing in a crop of young players, teaching them the game, and offering enjoyable places to play. The New York City Parks Department is making a contribution of its own—an unusual public outdoor table with an all-weather surface near Stuyvesant High School. Here a city worker demonstrates the game to an all-girl team in the shadow of the World Trade Center. Outdoor pool is ubiquitous in China but almost unknown in the United States. Wind, dust, rain and bird droppings make playing a serious game difficult, but there's little to compare with running a rack in the fresh air on a beautiful day right next to the Hudson River.

THE MEN

For more than a hundred years, the
United States has produced collectively the finest professional pool players on Earth. The notion that they were the best was essentially unchallenged until the late 1980s, when a few European and Oriental players made their mark in world competition, particularly Efren Reyes (Philippines), Oliver Ortmann (Germany) and Ralf Soquet (Germany). However, taken as a whole the Americans dominate the rest of the world in Eight-Ball, Nine-Ball and Straight Pool.

The first billiard tournament held in the United States was in 1860. Through the Civil War, as much coverage was devoted to billiard competition in the major newspapers as war news. National-level pool tournaments began in 1878, and for the next ninety years national and world competition was conducted in the United States almost without interruption, even during wartime. In the nineteenth century, billiards was the primary male amusement in the United States. Right

Left to right:

George Breedlove

Ismael Paez

Tony Ellin

Rodney Morris

Max Eberle

Opposite:

Dan Louie

and they lacked a strong organization to represent and protect them. At the same time, the quality of their play increased tremendously. In the 1970s the principal tournament game shifted from Straight Pool to Nine-Ball, a faster game more suited to television. The result was an improvement in Nine-Ball technique never before seen, particularly the refinement of the jump shot.

In 1991, the Professional Billiards Tour (PBT) was formed to promote the interests of the male professionals and provide them with a steady stream of tournaments from which to draw income. However beneficial its original goals may have been, the PBT grew insular and despotic. It refused to let its members participate in non-PBT events, rejected the role of the BCA as governing body of pool and set its own course. The inability of PBT players to choose the events in which they would play may have been satisfactory for the top echelon of money winners, but the mid-rank pros were unable to make enough from the PBT since they were prevented from earning other income. C. J. Wiley,

C. J. Wiley is one of the best, most colorful and controversial figures in modern pool. He owns C. J.'s Billiard Palace, a large emporium in Dallas, and is one of the games' leading money winners. He bit the hand that fed him, however, in forming the PCA. The Reno tournament was a showdown of sorts between the PBT and its younger cousin, the PCA, of which Wiley is President. He did not play well, possibly because of distractions over the future of the PCA. Here he is watching a game at an adjacent table instead of concentrating on his next shot.

a Texas professional who rose to the level of board member of the PBT, felt that the board had no real power and was being left in the dark on financial matters. This situation led Wiley to quit in 1995 to form the rival Professional Cuesports Association (PCA).

The theory of the PCA was that its members would be free to participate in any events they chose, provided that they also played in PCA tournaments. PBT members were entreated to jump ship to the PCA, and some famous names, including Earl Strickland, did so. PBT players were banned from PCA events, and the usual symptoms of internecine rivalry broke out. In 1996, the PBT had its best year ever, with the highest total winnings for American pool players in history, thanks to the sponsorship of R. J. Reynolds and its Camel brand. The PCA also began strongly. Its tournaments offered a standing prize of one million dollars to any player who could run ten consecutive racks of Nine-Ball without his opponent getting a shot. In its very first tournament, in 1996, Strickland ran 11 racks and claimed the prize.

Johnny Archer, one of the country's top-ranked players, eyes opponent Tommy Kennedy intently during their match. Archer is one of a handful of players who has run 150 points in a 150-point tournament game of Straight Pool.

Davenport breaking in the first game of the finals (far right). The cue stick bends because he shoots downward into the cloth. Because of the stress on the shaft and joint during the break shot, most professionals use a separate cue just for the break shot to avoid damage to their regular cue. Note that Davenport's break cue has a light-colored butt; his playing cue (right) is dark.

George San Souci and Kim Davenport lag for break. San Souci uses a classic stance, with the cue stick directly under his chin; Davenport plays slightly sidearm, with the grip hand held away from the body. Sidearm shooting is characteristic of players who began at a very young age, when they were too short both to sight the ball and hold the cue beneath the head at the same time. Although regarded as a flaw in technique, the shortcomings of sidearm shooting can easily be overcome through experience, as in Davenport's case.

During the 1930s, a national pool tournament would usually last three weeks. This was during the Depression, when many people had time on their hands. Matches were held twice a day—one in the afternoon and one in the evening. These days, neither players nor spectators can devote more than a few days to a tournament, so many games are played simultaneously, particularly in the early rounds until the number of competitors dwindles.

By 1997, both the PBT and the PCA were in financial distress. As of the beginning of the year, the PBT owed its players $400,000 in unpaid purses, money that had been won over the table but never collected. The PCA was sent reeling by an insurance dispute—Strickland's million-dollar prize had never been properly insured and the PCA was unable to pay it. Then Reynolds withdrew its support from the PBT, leaving it without a viable tournament sponsor. Neither organization was able to promote a tournament for its members during 1997 that matched the prize money available the previous year.

It is understandable if the men are disaffected. The best players in the world, they are not even assured of being paid for their victories. This is not to say that tournaments have vanished, but major ones have become rarer. One of the most reliable tournaments in history is the Sands Regency Open Nine-Ball event, which has been held twice a year in Reno, Nevada, since 1985. The motive force behind the event is Barbara Woodward (page 111), who creates a joyride for both players and spectators. The competition is truly open, without regard to gender. In June 1997, the 25th tournament in the series attracted 185 entries, including five women. This one was notable because it was

Top to bottom:

Davenport stands far back from the table to view the shot properly. Ball in hand situations are not as simple as they look because of the need to decide not only how to hit the cue ball, but also where to place it.

Davenport positions the cue ball carefully. He doesn't want it too far from the object ball, which would make the shot more difficult, but he doesn't want it too close either, because of the risk of hitting the cue ball twice, which is a foul that would lead to loss of turn.

The shot is in progress. The 2-ball has hit the 9, which is traveling toward the pocket. The cue ball is drawing back toward the left cushion. Davenport has had to withdraw his bridge hand from the table to avoid touching the returning cue ball. The 9-ball did not go in, however. It hit the side and end cushions and stopped in exactly the same place it had started! The safety portion of the shot was successful, though. San Souci was left without being able to see the 2-ball.

Top to bottom:

San Souci is forced to kick at the 2-ball. He hit it, but the cue ball scratched in a side pocket. The 2-ball rolled into a position only a fraction of an inch from where it was when Davenport missed the combination originally.

Davenport is faced with the same combination two innings in a row. He is determined not to miss again.

Davenport makes a small adjustment and plays the shot the same way, to leave safe in case of a miss. This time the 2-ball is going in exactly the right direction.

One of the psychological **agonies** of pool is that a player can do nothing when his opponent is shooting. In this it differs from most other sports. Even in purely offensive sports such as bowling and archery, one player by skill cannot prevent the other from participating at all. In pool, a player can theoretically win a match without his opponent ever having a chance to shoot.

The final shot of the tournament: with his family looking on, Davenport has positioned the cue ball perfectly and is dead straight on the 9-ball. San Souci, at rear, knows what is coming but is powerless to prevent it (overleaf).

men's tournaments

have been plagued for decades by promoters who have run events but failed to pay the winners. Sanctioning organizations formerly would not allow an event to take place unless the entire prize fund was deposited in a bank in escrow in advance. Such protection is only available when sanctioning bodies are strong, which is not presently the case in men's, as opposed to women's, pool. When a casino sponsors a tournament, prizes are always paid in full, which partly accounts for the popularity of such events among players. There is some chance, however, that a winner will be tempted to risk some of his gains on a variety of gaming opportunities before he has a chance to leave the casino.

Davenport and San Souci receive their prizes in cash on the spot from Linda Silva (left) and Barbara Woodward (right) of the Sands. It's a casino, after all.

Even though billiards has been played
for more than 500 years, modern billiard equipment dates only from the Industrial Revolution of the nineteenth century. Between 1815 and 1845, nearly every item of billiard technology now in use was developed, including slate table beds, rubber cushions, heated tables, the leather cue tip and the jointed cue. Shortly thereafter, in 1868, the plastic ball was invented by John Wesley Hyatt, who was inducted into the Hall of Fame for his contribution. In fact, the very purpose of plastic was to replace expensive and unreliable ivory billiard balls.

Players of every sport are obsessed with its equipment. Small differences in playing utensils can mean the margin between victory and defeat. In pool, the rebound of a ball from a cushion, the friction produced by cue chalk, the flex of a cue stick, the width of a pocket, the speed of the cloth and the roll of a table all affect a player's performance. So people who play regularly are always on the lookout for new products and improvements, which in turn feeds the cue manufacturers, table makers, chalk factories, lighting specialists, slate suppliers, cloth mills, retailers, room proprietors, clothing suppliers and pocket fabricators that together make up the billiard industry.

Every summer, the Billiard Congress of America holds its annual International Trade Expo where industry insiders introduce new products, forge alliances and conduct business at a brisk pace. The Expo is not open to the general public, so most pool fans never get to see the astonishing range of products that are available.

Many top players attend the Expo because (1) they love pool and are deeply involved in its promotion; and (2) they endorse products that are exhibited at the show. The mix of players, promoters, buyers, manufacturers, writers and room owners generates a pool spirit that lasts for three days—from the opening to the Hall of Fame Banquet, at which the year's inductee is honored and asked to take his or her place

A small part of the show floor at the
Sands Convention Center for the BCA
International Trade Expo in Las Vegas,
1997. The Expo is a cornucopia of pool
products, including cues, balls, tables,
books, pool room furniture, lighting and a
host of other items. Open only to the
industry, the show is a venue for business
deals, trick shot demonstrations, product
endorsements and manufacturers'
cocktail parties. The billiard industry is
relatively small, but everyone attends
the Expo (previous pages).

Cuemaker Paul Huebler of Paul Huebler
Industries writes up an order for a
buyer (left). Huebler is an industry legend
and former BCA President with a no-
nonsense attitude toward cues. His slogan:
"Get a Huebler or get beat by one!"

The cues shown here are Samsara
models, costing from one to several
thousand dollars each. Samsara, based
in New Hampshire, is known for its
distinctive designs and multicolored
woods (overleaf).

Sales of cues are always brisk, since every player wants one. By contrast, many people can share use of a table. When you go out to shoot, you don't bring your own table, but you do bring a cue. The spectrum and pricing of cues are very broad. A house cue (typically a one-piece cue offered to the public in a rack in a pool room) can be had for under $10.00, although it is advisable to spend more. At the other end of the range, a few cues a year sell for over $100,000. They're not antiques, but one-of-a-kind designs with precious materials and requiring intricate work.

The rise of expensive collectible cues is one of the strangest phenomena in billiard history. From 1850 until the 1970s, the cost of billiard equipment remained essentially level after adjustment for inflation. This includes tables, cloth, ivory balls, chalk, other accessories and cues. At the beginning of the 70s, a hundred dollars could buy a superior cue. The number of custom cuemakers was small. Many of them would simply start from stock one-piece catalog cues, cut them apart, install a joint, re-tip, wrap, ornament, balance and refinish them into fine playing instruments. As the well-known makers such as George Balabushka and Gus Szamboti passed away, the demand for their work began to increase, which led to a surge in prices. When buyers demonstrated a willingness to pay several thousand dollars for a cue, many craftsmen entered the market. But simple playing cues were not sufficient to draw the same kinds of prices for modern makers. So they made the cues more and more intricate, and prices rose even further. One exhibitor at the Expo reported that he sold out all of his $6,000 cues within three hours after the show opened. At that price, a cue costs substantially more than the best quality American table.

Now many collector cues are never used for playing—merely chalking the tip reduces the value substantially, to say nothing of putting a dent in the butt. So we have a situation in which the best cues can never be used for their intended purpose, and these are the most valuable. The only logical reason that a buyer would pay so much for a cue only to put it away without hitting a ball is that cues are now works of art and are produced and admired for that reason.

The appetite for cues has given rise to a whole subindustry. The part of the cue that wears out fastest is the tip. So there are tip manufacturers. Despite a century of trying, no one has found a better tip material than animal hide, principally leather. The tip has to

be glued on, so there are companies that make tip cement. Holding a tip in place while the glue sets requires a clamp, but the clamp can't mar the surface of the shaft, which players insist on keeping perfectly smooth. A variety of cue clamps are available, some of them very clever, but the simplest is a shaped piece of plastic and a rubber band, which is not a precision device but adequate for a road player on a budget.

The number of cuemakers is now so large that entire businesses are devoted just to supplying them with parts and equipment. Rare woods, joint screws, ferrules (to which tips are attached), collars (which surround the joint), butt caps (to protect the heavy end of the cue, which is frequently dragged along the floor), thread for wrapping grips (where the hand grasps the butt), rubber bumpers (to deaden the sound when the butt cap hits the floor), blanks (prefabricated spliced pieces with triangular points that are difficult to make), veneers (thin strips of colored wood to enhance the appearance of points), inlays (small ornaments to embellish the appearance of a cue) and computer-controlled milling machines are all offered.

And that's not all. Special solvents and waxes are made for cleaning shafts. Tools can be had for removing nicks and dents. A cue has a joint at which it is screwed together. Joints can become dirty or damaged, so joint protectors are sold to prevent this from happening. Once you take out your cue, you need a place to store it, hence the profusion of cue racks and cue holders.

You can't carry a cue without a case, a need met by a number of specialists. One question the consumer faces is whether to pay more for the case that the cue cost originally. Sometimes the case, whether in hand-tooled leather or inlaid wood, is just as artistic a production as a cue stick. Yet other case hounds seek out exotic skins, such as snake, ostrich or elephant. A casual player might be satisfied with one that holds a single butt and a single shaft (called a 1 x 1). A league player might require a 1 x 2 (for one butt and two shafts). Someone who owns three cues (the maximum number that can be brought to the table under the official rules) would ask for a 3 x 6. Tournament and exhibition players need cases that hold a large selection of cues. Cue salesmen need demonstration cases that hold butts only, and the list goes on.

Once the tip is attached, it has to be shaped and maintained, so there is a dizzying variety of cutters, burnishers, trimmers, tappers and scuffers available. Cue repair is a valuable and necessary service. Some shops set up booths at trade shows and tournaments with lathes for fast and accurate re-work. Ted Harris (right) is said by pro players to be one of the best. There are even repair services that operate entirely by mail.

Some cues are so expensive that their owners constantly invite burglary. The Cue Safe Co. of Chicago is perhaps ahead of its time with a special collector's vault for storing designer sticks along with bearer bonds, certificates of deposit and other trappings of extreme wealth. Humor aside, safes were once common in pool rooms for safekeeping of expensive ivory balls.

BCA
INTERNATIONAL
TRADE
EXPO

1300-1400

For more than a century, pool in the United States has been bound up with the fortunes of the Brunswick Corporation and its predecessors, notably the Brunswick-Balke-Collender (BBC) Company. It began in 1845 when an immigrant Swiss carriage maker, John Brunswick, decided to use his skills to make fine billiard tables. Through a series of mergers, the company grew huge by the 1880s. Its output of billiard tables was so large that it not only owned its own sawmills to feed its factories, but even owned the forests from which the trees were felled for the mills. By 1910, privately held BBC was in complete control of tournament billiards in the United States. None of its competitors was even a minor annoyance. All major players were under contract to BBC and, in return for comfortable lives, were required to do the company's bidding. Even the world champion did not have enough clout to buck this arrangement. BBC lobbied for laws favorable to the industry and even got the New York State Legislature to make it illegal to use the word "pool" in naming or advertising a billiard room because it felt the word had unpleasant connotations.

In 1960, BBC was absorbed into a huge conglomerate and became Brunswick Corporation. Billiards then formed only a small part of its business, and the fortunes of the industry, though buoyed by the film *The Hustler* in 1961, began to decline. After *The Color of Money* was released in 1986, the game revived quickly and upscale rooms began to spring up. This created a new demand for tables, and Brunswick Billiards, now a separate division, began to grow.

Nearly every table requires a slate bed. (Some inexpensive models use substitutes of various kinds, but are unsatisfactory except for casual use.) Slate for billiard tables became widespread after 1830, when machinery was

Connelly Billiards stacked ten of its tables to form a pyramid with a shipping weight of over 15,000 pounds.

invented for cutting and smoothing it. Suitable slate can be found, however, in only one place in the world—Italy, particularly Liguria, near Genoa. Some slate is also quarried in Vermont and South America, but is not preferred by table makers. This gives the Italians something of a monopoly, and numerous efforts have been made over the last 150 years to find an effective alternative to slate. Marble, granite, steel, wood, aluminum and a variety of honeycomb materials have been tried, without success. The bed must be heavy, resilient, porous (to avoid a buildup of moisture under the cloth), flexible (so it can settle into a level shape by force of gravity) and readily machinable and transportable. Slate is the only plentiful substance known that has even a majority of these properties.

The Italians are always a major presence at the Trade Expo. So intimately tied to billiard tables are the Italian slate quarries that the health of the billiard industry in a given country can be measured by the volume of slate orders received in Italy from that country.

Billiard tables have been covered with cloth since the mid-fifteenth century. Until 50 years ago, the universal color was green. Since then, cloth color has become a decorator choice and only purists continue to insist on green. The rules do not require any specific color, and everything from white to black and even patterned cloth has been sold. It is believed that the ideal color for players is one that does not induce eye fatigue, but also one in which the outline of the balls can be easily distinguished. This suggests a dark color not similar in shade to any ball, for example, brown or gray. Black is no good because the 8-ball vanishes when it is used. Green is not ideal for pool (though it may be for carom games) because the 6-ball is solid green. However, there is little chance of dislodging green because of its overwhelming popularity.

Much more important than the color of a cloth are its playing characteristics, which are determined by its thickness, thread content, weave and finish. A "fast" cloth is one on which the balls roll quickly. The fastest cloths are used for Three-Cushion Billiards, because of the great

the industry

That Italians play a game called "Cinque Birilli" or **five-pins**. Five small pins, shaped like bowling pins but made of plastic (formerly wood), are placed on predefined spots near the center of the table. The game is played on a regular ten-foot carom table with heavy cues (weighing up to 26 ounces as opposed to the usual weight for pool games of 18 ounces). Two cue balls are used, a yellow and a white, each belonging to one of the players. The object is to hit your cue ball into the other player's cue ball, and that cue ball must knock down one or more pins to score points. The game is unique in that each player is allowed only a single shot per inning, regardless of the outcome. That means that every shot is both offensive and defensive; you have to score points without leaving the balls in a position from which the opponent can score more. The game is delicate and beautiful, with the balls traveling long distances often very slowly. Five-Pin enjoys a huge following in Italy and South America. Tournament purses vastly exceed those of any U.S. pool event, and several Italians earn more from each Five-Pin contest than the top American pool player makes in a year.

Rolls of Granito cloth made from 100 percent worsted wool of a quality that can be (and often is) used to make fine men's suits.

distance the cue ball must travel during a shot. A cloth that is too fast is not good for pool, because the speed makes it almost impossible to play precise position—it is difficult to hit the cue ball softly enough to stop it in the desired place. The two best-known cloth makers internationally are Simonis of Belgium and Granito of Spain. While billiard cloth is often referred to as "felt," even inexpensive cloths never contain felt, which is not woven and would not survive an evening of 9-ball.

The cloth of a table is an organic substance which, although not living, breathes and is able to absorb and discharge moisture. On a humid day, a thick cloth will slow noticeably as the fibers absorb water from the air. To maintain consistent playing conditions, European table manufacturers install a heating element beneath the slate to raise the temperature of the table about nine degrees above room temperature. This drives moisture from the cloth so play is not affected by changes in humidity. It also feels good to play on a warm table.

Cloth gets dirty, so it needs to be cleaned. We vacuum floors even though we never do more

In 1997, the Italians favored the United States by conducting the finals of a Five-Pin tournament on the trade show floor at the Expo. They came equipped with television cameras, a tuxedoed referee and a bevy of officials. Here the shooter, using the yellow ball as his cue ball, attempts to bank the white ball across the table through the cluster of pins. The red ball serves only as an obstacle. The most expensive modern tables in the world are Italian carom models, because of their extremely thick slates and gorgeous woodwork. This one is by MBM Biliardi, owned by Mariano Maggio, a dapper gentleman who has served as President of Italy's National Billiard Union, the counterpart to the BCA (top).

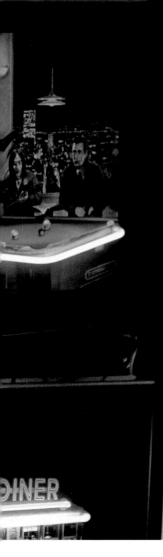

The importance of **lighting** in a pool room is often underestimated. The range of allowable illumination at the cloth under international rules is very narrow, varying from only 520 to 600 lux over the entire surface of the table, a tolerance of about 13 percent. If you walk into a pool room with a light meter, aside from receiving some strange looks and an icy reception from the proprietor, you'll rarely find a table that meets the standard. You can often see a drop-off in brightness of 75 percent at the corner pockets, which means you'd better shoot for the sides. While it should be no surprise that people need to see in order to aim, word of this has not spread as widely as one would like. Some rooms deliberately keep the table lights low to produce a more romantic atmosphere. If their patrons are interested in activities better performed in the dark, perhaps pool is not the recreation that should be offered.

Pool rooms need decoration, which the billiard industry is ready to provide. Aside from prints, posters, bar stools, clocks, cue racks and related paraphernalia, your room can be highlighted in ever-tasteful neon.

than walk on them. The bed of a billiard table is the entire playing arena and must be groomed just as much as a tennis court or golf green. Unwanted debris on the table interferes with the movement of the balls. Even a tiny piece of chalk can make a slowly moving ball deviate from its path and miss a pocket completely. Chalk dust on the cloth is quickly picked up by static electricity on the balls.

All of the work required to assemble tables and cues, weave cloth and ship slate halfway across the world is to no avail unless decent balls are available. The most skillful shot will go astray if a balls rolls off line at the last moment. The search for acceptable ball materials has gone on for centuries. Initially made of hard wood, balls of ivory began to be used in the eighteenth century. Ivory is difficult to obtain, expensive and temperamental. A quick change in temperature can cause a ball to shatter. Being essentially a tooth material, ivory has a natural grain along which the balls tend to warp and pick up veins of chalk dust. Using elephant tusks for billiard balls is shockingly inefficient; a single tusk weighing hundreds of pounds can be expected to yield only three billiard balls weighing little more than a pound. △

cleaning balls is a persistent problem in billiard rooms. Billiard paraphernalia should remain clean not only for the sake of appearance, but because its performance is affected by dirt, dust and other foreign substances. The rules require the referee to monitor the status of the equipment used in a game and to "clean any visibly soiled ball."

Ball cleanliness in many pool rooms is indifferent at best. Patrons take little care with equipment that is not their own and tend to be liberal in their use of both cue chalk and talcum powder. A tiny amount of chalk at the point of contact between two balls alters their angle of rebound considerably. So pronounced is the effect that there are trick shots in the repertoire that cannot be made unless chalk is surreptitiously applied to the balls. The "egg trays" in which most rooms store sets of balls are also used to hold cubes of chalk, and it is here that the infestation begins. Look in one of the trays sometime. The bottom will be dusted with blue chalk dust. Even rooms that clean the balls overlook the need to wash the egg trays.

Cleaning balls is not easy. If done by hand, it is tiresome and time-consuming. Machines have been made that roll the balls against a carpet-like surface to remove dirt and apply polish at the same time. These devices are effective for lightly soiled balls but are of scant use on ground-in chalk. Joe Porper set out to build a better ball cleaner. His machine rubs the balls on top and bottom while causing them to rotate both against other balls and cleaning surfaces, exposing every part of the surface of each ball to more cleaning action per second than other machines.

In order to attract people to their trade show booths, table makers hire trick shot artists to give exhibitions. One of the most dedicated and flamboyant of them is Tom "Dr. Cue" Rossman. He and his wife, Marty ("Ms. Cue"), log 50,000 miles a year giving exhibitions and teaching clinics at colleges and military posts. Booking between 200 and 300 shows a year is a full-time job for Marty. Tom's show is a fast-paced mixture of fun, skill and surprise. Here he illustrates an unusual but legal stance. Tom often makes wing shots (in which the object ball is moving when it is struck by the cue ball) in this position. Tom is an Artistic Billiards player as well as a BCA Certified Instructor. In 1997 he tied for first place in the North American Trick Shot Championship sanctioned by TASA, the Trickshot and Artistic Shooter's Association.

"Fast" Eddie Parker of Universal City, Texas, carefully sets up a trick shot by tapping the balls into place.

Sammy Jones, husband of women's champion, Loree Jon Jones, is one of the best jump shooters in the world. He has one of the fastest strokes of any professional (regularly clocked at over 30 miles per hour), and gives an eye-popping display of shaft jumping. In this shot sequence, Jones uses the shaft alone to launch the cue ball over eight intervening object balls to complete a combination on the two balls nearest the opposite corner pocket.

One of the few significant improvements in billiard technique developed in the last 40 years has been the **shaft jump** This is a method, now illegal in regular competition, in which the cue ball is struck using just the shaft of the cue.

A cue shaft does not weigh much more than a cue ball. Therefore, if the shaft is thrown at the ball from above in a controlled fashion, the shaft bounces back away from the ball, allowing the cue ball to jump rapidly without bouncing into the cue tip. Not only is immense loft possible this way, but the cue ball can be made to clear an object ball completely from a distance of a quarter of an inch.

Jumping with specialized cues became so highly developed that a rule was adopted in 1994 specifying that a cue stick must have a minimum length of 40 inches. A typical shaft is usually no more than 29 inches long, so the stroke is no longer permitted in tournaments.

Jerry Briesath is the dean of U.S. pool instructors, legendary for his ability to analyze and improve the fundamentals of even the best players. He established The Pool School in Madison, Wisconsin, was instrumental in setting up the BCA Certified Instructor program and is himself a Certified Master Instructor, the highest possible level, attained by only seven other people. Here Jerry checks the stance of Kathy Burghoffer, a league player out of Charlie's Lounge in Creston, Missouri, who reports tremendous improvement from having attended Jerry's course, the "College of Pool Knowledge." Jerry's tie, the glory of which does not come through fully in black and white, consists of a repeated image of Mickey Mouse playing pool.

One of the high points of the Trade Expo is the **Hall of Fame** ceremony at which the current inductee is honored. The BCA Hall of Fame is one of the most selective in all of sports. Since 1967, it has seen fit to enshrine only 37 individuals, many of them posthumously. Potential candidates are screened by a committee representing players, manufacturers and journalists. A ballot of at most five candidates is proposed, from which at most two can be elected by the BCA voting membership. In most years there is only one inductee.

Thousands of wheelchair players participate in Eight-Ball leagues. Special rules have been adopted by the BCA to accommodate wheelchair play that differs as little as possible from the standard rules. It is doubtful whether a good ambulatory amateur would have a chance against the best of the wheelchair players.

Players with **physical challenges** have been successful at billiards for at least a century. During World War II, severely injured British soldiers, who in some cases were unable to use their arms at all or even sit upright, became skilled at shooting with their feet while lying on hospital gurneys. One of the most amazing examples of such billiard prowess was George "Handless" Sutton, who lost both arms below the elbow in a sawmill accident while in his twenties. He became so good at carom billiards that he was able to beat even top amateurs 100 or no count, meaning that Sutton had to make at least 100 points in a single inning to score any points at all. A run of 99 counted as zero. Though his challenger was under no such restriction, Sutton would still win. He could play massé shots with or without a cue, in the latter case by spinning the cue ball between the stumps of his arms. Such a performance may seem macabre, but Sutton gave numerous public exhibitions and was anything but pitiable. Movie footage of his demonstrations survives to prove that his attitude and dexterity were awe inspiring.

At the beginning of 1996, John Fargo, owner of Gold Crown Billiards in New London, Connecticut, had a problem. He was a busy man, divorced, working as a full-time fire fighter, running a pool room and teaching pool in a local tavern to help his Bud Lite league. Then a mutual friend introduced him to Linda Schwartz, another player in the same league, and Fargo's troubles began to subside. The two hit it off, and before long Schwartz was hired to manage Fargo's room. They eventually decided to get married, but logistical problems made it difficult to set a date when both families could get together in the same city.

In July 1997, Schwartz and Fargo were heading out to Las Vegas to attend the Expo. They knew how easy it was to get married in Nevada, and traveled there with the idea of simplifying the process by holding their wedding in a hotel. During the plane ride, though, Fargo suggested that since they had to visit the Brunswick Billiards booth the next day, they might ask permission to marry right there.

On Thursday, July 17, they raised the idea with their sales representative, Judy Peterson, who discussed it with her management. James Knox, the President of Brunswick Billiards, was delighted, and offered the company's full support. The Sands Convention Center, site of the Expo, was alerted, and within four hours the entire wedding was planned and a minister contacted. The knot was tied on Friday afternoon, with no prior announcement. The best man was Steve Kapetan, the "best woman," Donna Shruga. The first bridesmaid on the left is Ewa Laurance; the usher at the extreme right is Jimmy Caras, a five-time world champion and endorser of Brunswick products for over 50 years.

The table in the photograph is Brunswick's beautiful Black Crown, which now sees service as the front table at Fargo's New London room. The couple spent their honeymoon in Vegas and even shot some pool. Getting married under an archway of cue sticks at a commercial trade show shows a dedication to the game that, while extreme, is not uncommon in the world of pool.

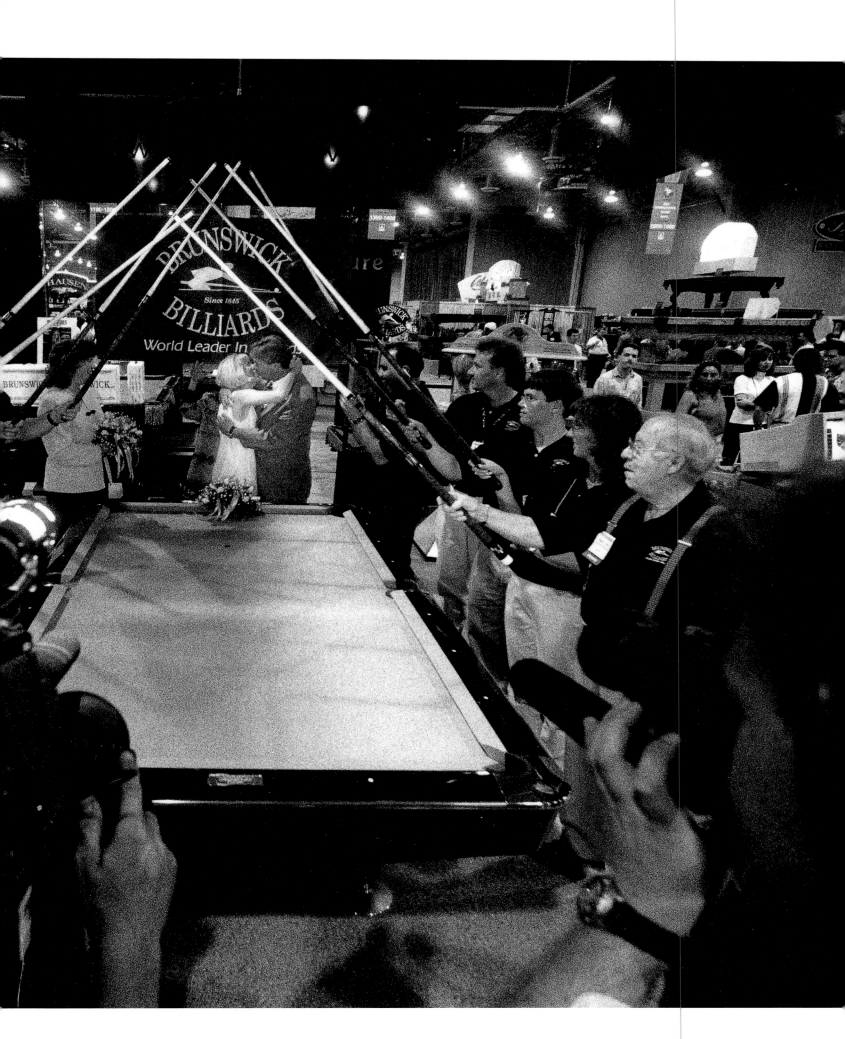

GLOSSARY

The list below is not a general pool glossary, but includes only the terms used in this book. A comprehensive selection of more than 2,000 billiard terms can be found in the author's *Illustrated Encyclopedia of Billiards* (Lyons & Burford, 1993).

action room A room where gambling can readily be found, generally frequented by serious players.

ACU-I The Association of College Unions—International, sponsor of intercollegiate competition in the United States.

Artistic Billiards A style of carom competition, popular in Europe, based on a set program of 68 fancy shots having numerical degrees of difficulty ranging from 4 (easiest) to 11. Each shot involves great skill and often requires application of extreme English, as by massé. This style of play is totally alien to the United States and no tournament has even been held here, although a small band of aficionados roam the country practicing the shots and damaging tables everywhere.

ball in hand The right of a player, following the opponent's foul or scratch, to position the cue ball anywhere on the playing surface of the table (except in contact with an object ball).

bank shot In pool, a shot in which the cue ball hits an object ball and that object ball contacts a cushion before entering a pocket. Contact with the cushions immediately adjacent to the pocket does not count; a shot in which the ball nudges a cushion as it is going into a pocket is not a bank shot.

bar table A smaller table, usually seven feet long, operated by inserting coins, often found in taverns.

BCA See Billiard Congress of America.

Billiard Archive A nonprofit historical foundation in Pittsburgh, Pennsylvania, that maintains a large collection of books, prints, photographs, cues, newspaper articles and artifacts related to pool, billiards and Snooker.

Billiard Congress of America (BCA) The governing body of billiards and pool in the United States, a member of the United States Confederation of Billiard Sports, which in turn belongs to the World Confederation of Billiard Sports, which is recognized by the International Olympic Committee. The BCA

sponsors various billiard organizations, promotes the game, assists room owners, and conducts educational and certification programs. It holds an annual International Trade Expo in Las Vegas and Orlando in alternating years.

billiards The generic term for any game played on a table with billiard balls, whether or not the table has pockets, and therefore includes pool. In specialized usage, billiards also refers to the pocketless forms of the game, especially Three-Cushion Billiards.

bridge The formation of the hand that supports the shaft of the cue stick during a shot. See mechanical bridge, open-hand bridge.

break shot The opening shot of a game. In Nine-Ball, the 1-ball must be contacted first on the break. If any ball is pocketed, the breaker continues shooting, otherwise the opponent takes over. In Straight Pool, the break shot is either the opening shot of the game or the shot taken at the beginning of a rack when the 15th ball of the previous rack remains on the table and the other 14 are racked to enable the player to continue shooting.

butt The thicker portion of a two-piece cue that is grasped by the hand to provide forward movement. See shaft.

carom The act of making one ball hit two others. In billiards, as opposed to pool, games, points are awarded for making caroms under various conditions. In pool, the carom shot is a legal way of pocketing a ball.

carom table A table without pockets, usually ten feet long, used for carom games.

Certified Instructor An instructor, either at the Recognized, Certified, Advanced or Master Instructor Level, who has experience as a teacher and has undergone a course of training and testing prescribed by the BCA.

Cinque Birilli See Five-Pin.

Classic Tour The professional tour operated by the WPBA.

combination A shot in which the cue ball hits an object ball and that object ball causes a different object ball to be pocketed.

cue ball A ball that may be struck directly with the tip of the cue stick, as opposed to an object ball, which may not. Cue balls vary in weight (and therefore moment of inertia) and some are believed superior to others to the extent that some players travel with their own cue ball rather than rely on those supplied by the room owner.

draw Backspin applied to the cue ball by striking below its vertical center, generally causing the cue ball to move backward after contacting another ball.

Eight-Ball The most popular pool game in the world. All 15 balls are racked in a triangle. The player who first pockets a ball legally is entitled to select a "group," either the solids (numbered 1–7) or the stripes (9–15). The player who first legally pockets the 8-ball after all balls of his or her group are pocketed is the winner. Eight-Ball is particularly suited for bar tables because no ball other than the cue ball ever needs to be returned to the table should it be pocketed or accidentally leave the table during a game. Eight-Ball, though often played by novices, is a positional game requiring great skill and is a challenge even for top professionals.

English Spin imparted to the cue ball by striking somewhere other than its center. Some sources insist that only right and left spin (as opposed to follow and draw) are properly called English.

Five-Pin A European and South American carom game played with three balls supplemented with five small pins in the shape of bowling pins arranged near the center of the table. The idea is to drive one ball into another and have the second ball knock over one or more pins. A unique feature of the game is that each player is allowed only one shot in each turn at the table, whether or not a score results. Thus each shot is both offensive and defensive. In Italian, *Cinque Birilli*.

follow Overspin applied to the cue ball by striking above its vertical center, generally causing the cue ball to continue forward after contacting another ball.

front table The most visible table in a room, usually near the front door, on which players who like to be seen compete. Called by Chalkers's owner Sue Backman a "show-off table."

Hall of Fame An entity maintained by the BCA to honor great players and people who have made major contributions to the game of billiards. Through 1997, only 37 people, including three women, had been inducted.

house pro A player, usually a touring pro, who is responsible for instruction in a pool room and often has such ancillary responsibilities as running a pro shop, maintaining equipment and organizing leagues.

hustler Technically, a player who disguises his real ability in order to trap unwary suckers into incautious betting. Often, but erroneously, used by the public to mean someone who plays for money rather than love.

joint The portion of a two-piece cue stick where the shaft and butt are joined, usually with a screw made of metal or wood.

jump shot A shot in which the cue ball is made to rise from the cloth and spend part of its trajectory aloft, usually to leap over an intervening ball.

kick A shot in which the cue ball strikes a cushion before another ball.

lag A process by which the opening break of a match is awarded to one of the contestants. The players each shoot a ball from one end of the table down to the far short cushion and back. The player whose ball comes to rest closest to the cushion from which they were shot is the winner and may elect to break or assign the break to the opponent.

mace An antique device that became obsolete more than a century ago, used for shoving the cue ball instead of striking it. The mace consists of a heavy block of wood manipulated by a handle mounted upward and at an angle so a player using it does not have to bend over. For centuries women were forced to use the mace to prevent them from tearing the cloth, which was easy to do with the untipped cues used before 1820.

massé A shot in which extreme spin is imparted to the cue ball by raising the cue stick to a nearly vertical position and striking downward and through the ball.

mechanical bridge A device resembling a rake on which the cue stick may be rested to make shots beyond a player's normal reach.

Nine-Ball The most popular professional pool game. The object balls 1–9 are racked in the shape of a diamond with the 1–ball on the foot spot and the 9-ball in the center of the diamond. On each shot, the player must first contact the lowest ball then remaining on the table. If a ball is legally pocketed, the player continues shooting. The player who first sinks the 9-ball legally is the winner. A player who commits fouls in three consecutive shots loses automatically. Nine-Ball is very fast and therefore usually played in sets, such as a race to nine. It gives rise to dazzling shots because of the need to position the cue ball properly for a specific ball on the next shot.

object ball Any ball other than a cue ball. In American pool games, a ball that may be legally pocketed. A ball that is never struck directly with the cue stick, except in unusual games not mentioned in this book.

One-Pocket The most psychologically harrowing of pool games. Played with a rack of 15 balls, the opening breaker chooses one of the two corner pockets nearest the rack as his. The opponent is assigned the other corner pocket. Any ball that enters one of these two pockets on a legal shot counts for the player who owns the pocket, regardless of who shot it. Balls entering any other pocket are respotted. To win, a player need have only eight balls to his credit, but it's not so easy. A single game can occupy 45 minutes, in which most of the shots are defensive. There is endless work in moving balls slowly toward one's pocket while leaving the cue ball positioned so the opponent can't knock them away, make a shot or move more balls toward his own pocket. Not a game for emotional weaklings, it is always played for money since no sane person would put himself through such torture for nothing.

open-hand bridge A bridge in which the cue stick is rested atop the fingers instead of being grasped as in a loop bridge.

PBT The Professional Billiards Tour. The dominant men's professional association, run by Commissioner Don Mackey and President Pat Fleming.

PCA The Professional Cuesports Association, formed by Dallas pro C. J. Wiley in 1995. A men's professional organization, rival to the PBT.

players' room A room that caters to serious players by providing superior equipment and table maintenance, a quiet atmosphere for high-stakes games and a see-no-evil attitude toward gambling.

pool Any billiard game in which scoring is accomplished only by pocketing balls. It originally referred to the collective bet, or "pool," anted by the players before the start of a game.

race A match format consisting of a series of individual games, the first player to win a predetermined number of games being the winner of the match. For example, the baseball World Series is a race to four. Nine-Ball matches are usually a race to seven, nine or eleven games. A race to n is always decided in at most $2n - 1$ games.

rack The arrangement of the object balls at the start of a game, consisting of 15 of them (in Eight-Ball) or 9 (in Nine-Ball). In Nine-Ball, a rack is synonymous with a game, as in, "She ran the next three racks."

railbird An intent spectator, so called because he "hangs on the rail" separating the audience from the playing area.

road player A player who attempts to make a living by traveling to rooms in which he is not known so he can create favorable betting situations.

room A pool hall, billiard room, bar or other location where pool and billiards are played.

run the table To sink all the remaining object balls on the table in consecutive shots without missing.

safe A defensive move in which a shot is missed deliberately to leave a difficult position for the opponent.

see A player can see a ball if there is an unobstructed path from the cue ball to some part of that ball.

set In pool, a series of games, usually in race format.

scratch A shot in which the cue ball enters a pocket, resulting in a foul.

shaft The thinner portion of a cue stick that narrows toward the tip, which contacts the cue ball during a shot.

shaft jump A jump shot, now illegal, performed by using only the shaft of a cue that has been detached from the butt.

Snooker A game, popular in the present and former countries of the British Commonwealth, played on a 12-foot table having narrow pockets with a cue ball and 21 object balls, 15 red and 6 of different colors. The object is to pocket reds and colors alternately, the colors being returned to the table by being placed at predefined spots. After all the reds have been pocketed, the colors are then pocketed in a particular order. Reds are worth one point each, the colors from two to seven points. The player with the greater number of points when all balls have been sunk is the winner. A characteristic feature of the game is that a foul results in points being added to the opponent's score. This leads to plays that are made purely for the purpose of scoring defensive points in this fashion.

Straight Pool A game played with a full rack of 15 balls and a cue ball. When a single ball remains on the table, the remaining 14 are racked and the player attempts to sink the lone ball and drive the cue ball into the other 14 to separate them so play can continue. Pocketing a ball is worth one point; the game continues until one player has reached a predetermined point total, usually 150. On any shot a player may sink any ball; there are no restrictions such as those in Eight-Ball and Nine-Ball. Straight Pool is serene and methodical. A game can last two hours rather than the five minutes often expended in Nine-Ball. The dominant professional game in the United States from 1911 until the 1970s, Straight Pool is now rarely played because a single player may occupy the table for a long period of time, which gives the mistaken impression that the game is not competitive.

table time The charge imposed by a billiard room for the use of a table.

Three-Cushion Billiards A sublime game invented in the 1870s and played on a 10-foot table with three balls and no pockets. A point is scored by causing the cue ball to contact both other balls, with the proviso that the cue ball must make at least three cushion contacts before hitting the second ball. The cushion contacts may occur in any order and may involve any number of cushions. For example, the cue ball may hit three cushions first, then touch both balls. Each carom is worth one point. The game is played to a preset number of points, usually 50, the first player to achieve this total being the winner. The game is difficult; the best player in the world, Torbjorn Blomdahl of Sweden, on the average has only a two out of three chance of making a shot. For most excellent players the chance is less than 50 percent; an amateur would be happy with a probability of one out of three.

tied up A Nine-Ball situation in which a player cannot make the cue ball contact the lowest numbered ball on the table directly. A player who is tied up must usually resort to a kick or jump shot.

upscale room A room in which decor and a high-budget atmosphere are priorities. These amenities result in a corresponding increase in table rates, but you get what you pay for.

wing shot An exhibition shot, not legal in competition, in which the player pockets a ball that is still moving.

WPBA The Women's Professional Billiard Association, formed in 1976 to promote women's professional pool.

Abel's Club (room), 81

Aguero, Billy, 11, 13, 14

Alaska, 76

Aliquippa, Pa., 76

Allen and Dawn Hopkins's
Super Billiards Expo, 40

American Billiard School, 17

Ames Billiards (room), 64

Amsterdam Billiards (room),
90

Annigoni, Tony, 62, 64–65

Anson, Cap, 74

Aravena, Rolando, 90

Archer, Johnny, 29, 101

Astor, Mrs. Vincent, 35

Astoria, N.Y., 81

Atkisson, Andee, 122–23

Backman, Sue, 13–14

Balabushka, George, 117

Balsis, Joe, 19

Balukas, Al, 25

Balukas, Jean, 17, 24–27, 36–39

BCA (Billiard Congress of
America), 100, 115, 116–17, 133

BCA Certified Instructor, 17,
130, 132

BCA Hall of Fame, 19, 23, 25,
132

BCA Trade Expo, 29, 134

Bellflower, Calif., 47

Billiard and Bowling Institute
of America, 23

Billiard Congress of America,
see BCA

Billiard Encyclopedia, The
(Stein), 76

Billiard Palace (room), 47

Billiards Digest, 14, 17, 23

Billing, Billie, 39

Blatt, Ron, 30–31

Blatt, Sam, 31

Blatt Billiards, 30–31

Blue Fin Cafe and Billiards
(room), 64–68

Boca Raton, Fla., 74–75

Boston, Mass., 56

Bow Tie Billiards (room), 68

Breakers (room), 62, 86

Breedlove, George, 47, 98

Brenner, David, 90

Bridgeville, Pa., 86–87

Briesath, Jerry, 132

Brooklyn, N.Y., 23, 24

Brunswick, John, 123

Brunswick-Balke-Collender
Company, 55, 123

Brunswick Billiards, 123, 134

Brunswick Corporation, 123

Brunswick New York Classic
(tournament), 90

Brunswick tables, 25, 31, 61, 76

Brunswick World Open (tournament), 25

Burghoffer, Kathy, 132

Byrd, Palmer, 39

Calderone, Abel, 81

Calvert, J. R., 85

Caras, Jimmy, 19, 134

Chalkers San Francisco (room),
13–15

Charlie's Lounge (room), 132

Chelsea Billiards (room), 88–89

Chesapeake, Va., 29

Chicago, Ill., 120

Chicago Cubs, 74

Cho, Sonny, 81

C. J.'s Billiard Palace (room),
100

Clean Shot Billiards, 129

Cochran's (room), 62

Color of Money, The (film), 94,
123

Connelly Billiards tables, 123

Connelly Classic (tournament),
36, 40

Corner Billiards (room), 16–17

Crane, Irving, 19

Crawford, Dan, 77

Creston, Mo., 132

Crimi, Fran, 16–17

Cruise, Tom, 94

Cue Safe Co., 120

Dallas, Tex., 100

Davenport, Kim, 102–11

de Jager, Hans, 74

DeMarco, Michael, 77

Denver, Colo., 129

Dodson, Robin Bell, 25–26,
40, 47

Douglas, Michael, 90

Drones Bar & Grill, 58

Duquesne Club, 77

Eberle, Max, 98

8 Ball (room), 71

Ellin, Tony, 94–97, 98

Elliott, LaMar, 129

Elmhurst, N.Y., 81

Emeryville, Calif., 13, 14

ESPN, 36–41

ESPN World Open (tourna-
ment), 47

Evans, Steve, 86

Ewa Mataya Pool Guide, The
(Laurance), 40

Fargo, John, 134–35

Fat Kat's (room), 72–73

Fisher, Allison, 26, 36–40,
44, 47–53, 90

Flushing, N.Y., 80

4 x 4 Billiards (room), 80

Franklin's Sporting Goods
(room), 76

Ginacue cues, 33

Gleason, Jackie, 64

Gold Crown Billiards (room),
134

Gold Rush Billiards (room), 72

Gotham Hall (room), 61

Granito cloth, 125

Gutierrez, Ernie, 11, 32–33

Half Moon Bay, Calif., 82–83

Hall of Fame Billiards (room),
24–27

Hangarter, Peter, 13

Hard Times (room), 54

Harris, Ted, 120–21

Healdsburg, Calif., 68–69

Herman, Maurice, 16

Hofstatter, Gerda, 40

Hollywood Athletic Club
(HAC) (room), 58–59

Hollywood Billiards (room),
62–63

Honolulu, Hawaii, 47

Hopkins, Allen, 53

Hopkins, Dawn, 53

Hoppe, Willie, 23, 77, 94

Horlor, George, 77

Huebler, Paul, 116–17

Hunt, Ethan, 90

Hustler, The (film), 33, 64,
94, 123

Hyatt, John Wesley, 115

Ismaili, Isa, 77

Italy, 125–26

Jillian's (room), 56–57

Johnston City, Ill., 33, 86

Jointed Cue (room), 83

Jones, Loree Jon, 40, 131

Jones, Sammy, 131

Julian's (room), 54, 89

Kang, Mike, 81

Kapetan, Steve, 134

Kennedy, Tommy, 101

Kling, Johnny, 74

Knights of the Green Table, 77

Knox, James, 134

Largo, Fla., 19

Lassiter, Luther, 19, 86

Las Vegas, Nev., 25, 29, 134

Laurance, Ewa Mataya,
40–43, 134

Laurance, Mitchell, 40

Ledman, Peg, 40

Lee, Edward, 77

Lee, Jeanette, 36–39, 47–51

Lee, Sang Chun, 56, 81

Le Q (room), 89

Lincolnwood, Ill., 56

Long Beach, Calif., 47, 56

Los Angeles, Calif., 62

Louie, Dan, 98–99

Loykasek, Mike, 68–69

McCumber, David, 62

McGinnis, Ruth, 36

Madison, Wis., 132

Maggio, Mariano, 125

Mannino, Nick, 29

Marino, Jimmy, 86–87

Martin, Ray, 18–21

Martin, Steve, 90

Mataya, Jimmy, 40

MBM Biliardi, 125

Meatball, Tony, 26

Meeker Vineyards, 68–69

Messier, Mark, 90

Miami, Fla., 72–73, 74

Miller Brewing Co., 23

Minneapolis, Minn., 13

Mizerak, Steve, 11, 22–23, 25

Mizrahi, Isaac, 61

Mizrahi, Rene, 60–61

Monterey, Calif., 64–68

Monterey Billiards (room), 68

Morris, Rodney, 98

Mosconi, Willie, 19, 23

Murphy, Cisero, 90

National Billiard Union, 125

Nebraska, 56

New London, Conn., 134

Newman, Paul, 64

New Wave Billiards (room), 74

New York, N.Y., 16–17, 30–31,
    77–79, 88–91, 94

New York Athletic Club, 77–79

New York City Parks
    Department, 90–91

New York Times Magazine, 40

99 Critical Shots in Pool, The
    (Martin), 19

North American Trick Shot
    Championship, 130

North Bay Pool League, 71

North Hollywood, Calif., 33

O'Hare, Nesli, 40

Old Princeton Landing (room),
    82–83

Orbach, Jerry, 90

Ortmann, Oliver, 93

Paez, Ismael, 98

Parker, "Fast" Eddie, 130

Paski, Vicki Frechen, 17

Paul Huebler Industries, 117

Pete Rose's (room), 74

Peterson, Judy, 134

Peter Vitalie Company, 122–23

Philadelphia, Pa., 58

Piñeres, Hernando, 74

Pink E's (room), 29

Pippin, Aileen, 40

Pittsburgh, Pa., 58, 62, 77, 84–86

Playing Off the Rail
    (McCumber), 62

Pool & Billiard Magazine, 19

Pool School, 132

Professional Billiards Tour
    (PBT), 14, 29, 94, 100–105

Professional Cuesports
    Association (PCA), 29,
    100–102

Professional Pool Players
    Association, 19

Q Club (room), 62

Queens, N.Y., 17, 47

Queens College, 17

Red's Recovery Room (room),
    70–71

Reno, Nev., 102

Reyes, Efren, 29, 93

Rhee, Danny, 81

Rice, Melissa, 17

R. J. Reynolds, 101–2

Rose, Pete, 74–75

Rossman, Marty "Ms. Cue," 130

Rossman, Tom "Dr. Cue," 130

Ruth, Babe, 74, 94

Sacramento, Calif., 83

Samsara cues, 117–19

San Antonio, Tex., 47

Sands Convention Center,
    111–17, 134–35

Sands Regency Open Nine-Ball
    (tournament), 102–13

Sands Regency Tournament,
    94–97

San Francisco, Calif., 13, 58,
    62–63

San Leandro, Calif., 14

San Souci, George "Ginky," 94,
    102–11

Santa Monica, Calif., 61

Santa Rosa, Calif., 72

Schwartz, Linda, 134–35

Seinfeld, Jerry, 90

Senior Tour, 23

Shepard, Laura, 84–85

Shooter's (room), 13

Shootz Cafe & Billiards
    (room), 84–85

Short, Martin, 90

Shruga, Donna, 134

Silva, Linda, 110–11

Simonis cloth, 13, 125

Simpson, David, 77

SL Billiards (room), 81

Sonoma County, Calif., 68–71

Soquet, Ralf, 93

Sorvino, Paul, 90

South Hills Golden Cue
    (room), 86–87

Stap, Mike, 77

Stein, Victor, 76

Stewart, Carly, 122–23

Stewart, Ron, 122–23

Stonier, Terry, 83

Strickland, Earl, 11, 28–29, 101

Sutton, George "Handless," 133

Szamboti, Gus, 117

Telluride, Colo., 13

Trickshot and Artistic Shooter's
    Association (TASA), 130

Universal City, Tex., 130

U.S. Open (tournament), 23, 25

U.S. Open Nine-Ball (tourna-
    ment), 14, 29

U.S. Open Straight Pool (tour-
    nament), 40

Valley Forge, Pa., 36, 40

Vanderbilt, Mrs. William, 35

Van Laare tables, 74

Varner, Nick, 19

Verhoeven tables, 81

Villarreal, Vivian, 40, 44–47

Vitalie tables, 31

Wagon Wheel Saloon (room),
    54–55, 71

Whitlow, Madeline, 39

Wiley, C. J., 29, 100–104

Wilhelmina tables, 74

Willie Hoppe Story, The (film),
    77

Willis, Bruce, 90

Women's Professional Billiard
    Alliance, 39

Women's Professional Billiard
    Association, *see* WPBA

Women's World Snooker (tour-
    nament), 47

Woodward, Barbara, 102, 110–11

World Three-Cushion
    Championship, 61

WPBA (Women's Professional
    Billiard Association), 17,
    39–40, 47

WPBA Classic Tour, 39, 47

WPBA Nationals, 17, 26

Ziesenheim, Frederick, 77

ACKNOWLEDGMENTS

acknowledgments

To Ray Martin, Steve Mizerak and Hernando Piñeres for being our first subjects on an early trip through Florida. Their participation enabled us to generate early enthusiasm for the book.

To Blatt Billiards, Ron Blatt and Barry Dubow for their hospitality and assistance.

To Elizabeth Holmes and Sue Backman for guided tours through northern California pool, in a few cases at some personal physical risk.

To Jay Helfert for arrangements, inspiration and help in the Los Angeles area. Anybody who rents a garage in another city just so he can have a place to shoot pool deserves all the support we can give him.

To Fran Crimi for insights into the process of pool instruction.

To The Billiard Archive in Pittsburgh, the country's largest repository of historical information about the game, for data about the evolution of pool in the United States.

To the Carom Billiard Foundation of America and President Deno Andrews for endorsing this project from its inception.

To the WPBA and its Executive Director, Mark Cord, for endorsing this project and inviting us to address the WPBA at the Connelly Classic at Valley Forge to encourage support for the book and granting us the right to photograph WPBA events.

To the PBT, Commissioner Don Mackey and President Pat Fleming for supporting the project and allowing us to photograph PBT players.

To PBT player and Shootz house pro J. R. Calvert for insights into the world of men's professional pool. To Shootz Cafe & Billiards and Manager Kristin Krebs for providing an oasis in which to play.

To the PCA and President C. J. Wiley for endorsing the project and granting permission to photograph PCA players.

To Barbara Woodward and the Sands Regency Reno for allowing us to cover the Sands Regency XXV tournament in Reno in June 1997.

To Dawn and Allen Hopkins for their cooperation in allowing us to photograph their Super Billiards Expo in Valley Forge.

To Bill Glasgow Sr., for access to the BCA International Trade Expo in Las Vegas.

To Bombay Gin, a libation so essential to survival in Las Vegas when the temperature was 108°F and the relative humidity an arid 9 percent.

To Bernard Holland and Leslie Stoker, for guidance and encouragement on this project.

To Mike Panozzo, publisher of *Billiards Digest* magazine, for hosting us at the BCA International Trade Expo.

To the memory of (Uncle) Bob Bowditch Sr., whose love for the game was an inspiration.

To our wives and families for exhibiting uncommon tolerance for our activities.

To all of our subjects, both willing and unwilling, who contributed to this mosaic of pool.

We thank you.

George Bennett
Mike Shamos